Acts of Faith

Acts of Faith

Edited by Jane Mead and Reid Sherline

TIMKEN PUBLISHERS

Published by Timken Publishers, Inc.
225 Lafayette Street, New York, NY 10012

LIBRARY OF CONGRESS CATALOGUING-IN-PUBLICATION DATA
Acts of faith : stories / edited by Jane Mead and Reid Sherline.
p. cm.
ISBN 0-943221-25-0 (paper)
1. Short stories. 2. Faith—Fiction. I. Mead, Jane, 1942– .
II. Sherline, Reid, 1962– .
PN6120.95.F17A27 1995
808.3'108382—dc20 95-21577
CIP

Typeset in Janson Text, with Bernhard Fashion and Skjald display
Designed and produced by David Bullen
Copyedited by Anna Jardine
Printed in the United States of America

Faith is the substance of things hoped for,
the evidence of things not seen.
EPISTLE TO THE HEBREWS, 11:1

Contents

Foreword

ALTHOUGH MANY OF the stories that follow may be considered "religious" because they explore spiritual characters or themes, this collection is not concerned with the existence of, or belief in, God. Faith here is considered more broadly—as any kind of belief that does not depend on logical proof or material evidence; that, indeed, requires the suspension of rational thought. As Frederick Buechner says in "Faith and Fiction," included here as an introduction, faith is "seeing and not seeing, seeing dimly, seeing from afar." For our purposes, that's what it is: reaching beyond the intellect to grasp that which cannot be held or seen.

The consequences of an act of faith may be grave (the old woman in Alice Walker's "The Welcome Table" sees Jesus on the road and walks with Him to her death) or not so grave (the narrator of Raymond Carver's "Cathedral" closes his eyes and learns to draw). Yet one thing is sure: Faith is almost always difficult. Beyond the difficulty lies an awakening—something that, for lack of a better word, might be called grace. The stories collected here recognize the difficulty of faith, the essential surprise of it, and the "grace" that is its reward. If faith were easy, it would be something else; it would be simply belief, or knowledge. If, for instance, the angel in Bernard Malamud's "Angel Levine" were a cherub with wings who descended from on high rather than a sloppily dressed black man reading a newspaper at the kitchen table, the story would be about not faith but divine revelation.

Because faith is often difficult, there are those who, no matter how hard they try, fail. Sometimes they are, oddly, the very ones whose vocation faith is supposed to be: the priest protagonists in Richard Bausch's "Design" and John L'Heureux's "The Expert on God" understand faith, yet it continues to elude them.

The stories emphasize one more thing, and that is the essential modesty—the smallness, as it were—of acts of faith. Faith is difficult, yes, but in fiction it is often achieved through small gestures rather than grand ones. Margarito Duarte, in Gabriel García Márquez's "The Saint," carries a small coffin containing the remains of his daughter, whom he believes to be a saint; in the end it is he who, for his quiet diligence, proves to be the saint. And there is Theresa, the protagonist of Francine Prose's *Household Saints*, whose "ordinary life [is] redeemed by extraordinary devotion."

The characters in all these stories are tested, to be sure. Yet more often than not their trials lie not in learning to be surprised by the miraculous, but in finding within themselves the ability to see the miraculous in the ordinary.

Frederick Buechner

Faith and Fiction

EXACTLY A YEAR ago tomorrow, the fifth of March, 1986, a very good friend of mine died. He was an Englishman—a witty, elegant, many-faceted man. One morning in his sixty-eighth year he simply didn't wake up. Which was about as easy a way as he could possibly have done it. But it wasn't easy for the people he left behind because it gave us no chance to say good-bye, either in words, if we turned out to be up to that, or in some unspoken way if we weren't. A couple of months later my wife and I were staying with his widow overnight in Charleston, South Carolina, when I had a short dream about him, which I want to tell you about.

I dreamed that he was standing there in the dark guest room, where my wife and I were asleep, looking very much the way he always did in the navy blue jersey and white slacks that he often wore, and I told him how much we missed him and how glad I was to see him again, and so on. He acknowledged that somehow. Then I said, "Are you really there, Dudley?" I meant was he there in fact and truth, or was I merely dreaming that he was? His answer was that he was really there. And then I said, "Can you prove it?" "Of course," he said. Then he plucked a strand of blue wool out of his jersey and tossed it to me, and I caught it between my index finger and my thumb, and the feel of it was so palpable and so real that it woke me up. That's all there was to the dream. But it was as if he had come on purpose to do what he had done and then left. When I told that dream at breakfast the next morning, I had hardly finished when my wife spoke. She said she had noticed the strand of wool on the carpet when she was getting dressed. She was sure it hadn't been there the night before. I thought I was losing my mind, and I rushed upstairs to see, and there it was—a little tangle of navy blue wool that I have in my wallet as I stand here today.

Another event was this. I went into a bar in an airport not long ago to fortify myself against my least favorite means of moving around the world. It was an off hour, so I was the only customer and had a choice of a whole row of empty barstools. And on the counter in front of each barstool there was a holder with a little card stuck in it, advertising the drink of the day, or something like that. I noticed that the one in front of me had an extra little bit of metal stuck on top of the card. It wasn't on any of the others, so I took a look at it. It turned out to be one of those tie clips that men used to wear. It had three letters engraved on it, and the letters were C.F.B. Those are my initials.

Lastly, this. I was receiving communion in an Episcopal church early one morning. The priest was an acquaintance of mine, and I could hear him moving along the rail from person to person as I knelt there waiting for my turn. The body of Christ, he said, the bread of heaven. The body of Christ, the bread of heaven. When he got to me he put in another word. The word was my name. "The body of Christ, Freddy, the bread of heaven."

The dream I had about my friend may very well have been just another dream, and you certainly don't have to invoke the supernatural to account for the thread on the carpet. The tie clip I find harder to explain away; it seems to me that the mathematical odds against its having not just one or two but all three of my initials and in the right order must be astronomical. But I suppose that too could be just a coincidence. On the other hand, in both cases there is also the other possibility. Far out or not, I don't see how any openminded person can *a priori* deny it. And it's that other possibility that's at the heart of everything I want to say here on this Ash Wednesday night.

Maybe my friend really did come in my dream, and the thread was a sign to me that he had. Maybe it's true that by God's grace the dead are given back their lives and that the doctrine of the resurrection of the body is not just a doctrine. My friend couldn't have looked more substantial, less ectoplasmic, standing there in the dark, and it was such a crisp, no-nonsense exchange that we had. There was nothing surreal or wispy about it.

As to the tie clip, it seemed so extraordinary that for a moment I almost refused to believe that it had happened. Even though I had the thing right there in my hand, with my initials on it, my first inclination was to deny it—for the simple reason that it was so unsettling to my whole common sense view of the way the world works that it was easier and less confusing just to shrug it off as a crazy fluke. We're all inclined to do that. But maybe it wasn't a fluke. Maybe it was a crazy little peek behind the curtain, a dim little whisper of providence from the wings. I had been expected, I was on schedule, I was taking the right journey at the right time. I was not alone.

What happened at the communion rail was different. There was nothing extraordinary about the priest knowing my name—I knew he knew it—and there was nothing extraordinary about his using it in the service because he evidently did that kind of thing quite often. But the effect on me was extraordinary. It caught me off guard. It moved me deeply. For the first time in my life, maybe, it struck me that when Jesus picked up the bread at his last meal and said, "This is my body which is for you," he was doing it not just in a ritual way for humankind in general, but in an unthinkably personal way for every particular man or woman or child who ever existed or someday would exist. Most unthinkable of all: maybe he was doing it for me. At that holiest of feasts we are known not just by our official name but by the names people use who have known us the longest and most intimately. We are welcomed not as the solid citizens that our Sunday best suggests we are, but in all our tackiness and tatteredness that nobody in the world knows better than each of us knows it about ourselves—the bitterness and the phoniness and the confusion and the irritability and the prurience and the half heartedness. The bread of heaven, *Freddy*, of all people. Molly? Bill? Ridiculous little So-and-so? Boring old What's-his-name? Extraordinary. It seemed a revelation from on high. Was it?

Maybe all that's extraordinary about these three little events is the fuss I've made about them. Things like that happen every day to everybody. They're a dime a dozen; they mean absolutely nothing.

Or, things like that are momentary glimpses into a mystery of such depth, power and beauty that if we were to see it head-on, in any way other than in glimpses, I suspect we would be annihilated. If I had to bet my life and my children's lives, my wife's life, on one possibility or the other, which one would I bet it on? If you had to bet your life, which would you bet it on? On "Yes, there is God in the highest," or, if that language is no longer viable, "There is mystery and meaning in the deepest"? Or on "No, there is whatever happens to happen, and it means whatever you choose it to mean, and that's all there is"?

Of course we can bet Yes this evening and No tomorrow morning. We may know we're betting; we may not know. We may bet one way with our lips, our minds, even our hearts, and another way with our feet. But we all of us bet, and it's our lives themselves we're betting with, in the sense that the betting is what shapes our lives. And of course we can never be sure we bet right because the evidence both ways is fragmentary, fragile, ambiguous. A coincidence, as somebody said, can be God's way of remaining anonymous, or it can be just a coincidence. Is the dream that brings healing and hope just a product of wishful thinking?

Or is it a message maybe from another world? Whether we bet Yes or No is equally an act of faith.

There's a famous section in the Epistle to the Hebrews where the author, whoever it was, says that "faith is the substance of things hoped for, the evidence of things not seen." Marvelous definition. Noah, Abraham, Sarah, all the rest, it goes on to say, all died in faith, not having received what was promised but having seen it and greeted it from afar, and having acknowledged that they were strangers and pilgrims on the earth. For such people make it clear that they're seeking a homeland. Wonderful passage.

In other words, faith, it seems to me, is distinctly different from other aspects of religious life and not to be confused with them, even though we often use the word "faith" to mean religious belief in general, as in the phrase "What faith are you?" Faith is different from theology because theology is reasoned and systematic and orderly, whereas faith is disorderly and intermittent and full of surprises. Faith is different from mysticism because mystics in their ecstasy become one with what faith can at most see only from afar, as that passage from Hebrews says. Faith is different from ethics because ethics is primarily concerned not, like faith, with our relationship with God but with our relationship with each other. I think maybe faith is closest to worship because, like worship, it is essentially a response to God. It involves the emotions and the physical senses as well as the mind. But worship is consistent, structured, single-minded and seems to know what it's doing, while faith is a stranger, an exile on the earth, and doesn't know for certain about anything. Faith is homesickness. Faith is a lump in the throat. Faith is less a position *on* than a movement *toward*—less a sure thing than a hunch. Faith is waiting. Faith is journeying through space and time.

So if someone (and this frequently happens) were to come up and ask me to talk about my faith, it's exactly that journey through space and time I'd have to talk about. The ups and downs of the years, the dreams, the odd moment, the intuitions. I'd have to talk about the occasional sense I have that life isn't just a series of events causing other events as haphazardly as a break shot in pool causes billiard balls to go off in many different directions, but that life has a plot the way a novel has a plot—that events are somehow leading somewhere. Whatever your faith may be, or my faith may be, it seems to me inseparable from the story of what has happened to us. And that's why I believe that no literary form is better adapted to the subject of faith than the form of fiction.

FAITH AND FICTION both journey forward in time and space and draw their life from that journey. They *are* that journey, really. They involve the concrete, the earthen, the particular, more than they do the abstract and the cerebral. In both faith and fiction the people you meet along the way, the things that happen to happen, the places—the airport bar, the room where you have a last supper with some friend—count for much more than ideas do. Fiction can hold opposites together in a story simultaneously, like love and hate, laughter and weeping, despair and hope, and so can faith, which by its very nature both sees and does not see. That's what faith is: seeing and not seeing, seeing dimly, seeing from afar. Probably its most characteristic utterance is that unforgettable one from the Gospel of Luke where a child is sick and Jesus says, "If you believe, I can heal him," and the man, speaking for everybody who has faith, says, "Lord I believe; help thou my unbelief." Opposites.

Faith and fiction both start once upon a time and are continually changing and growing in mood and intensity and direction. When faith stops changing and growing, it dies on its feet. And believe me, so does fiction when it stops growing and changing. And they have even more in common than that. They both start with a leap in the dark, to use that famous phrase. How can Noah or Abraham or Sarah or anyone else know for sure that the promise they die without receiving will be kept and that their journey in search of a homeland will ever get them home? How can anyone writing a novel or a story know for sure where it will lead and just how and with what effect it will end, or even if the story is worth telling? Let writers beware who from the start know too much about what they're doing and keep too heavy a hand on the reins. They leave too little room for luck, just as Abraham and Sarah, if they know too much about what they're doing as they live their stories, leave too little room for grace.

The word "fiction" . . . comes from a Latin verb meaning to shape, to fashion, to feign. That's what fiction does, and in many ways it's what faith does, too. You fashion your story as you fashion your faith, out of the great hodgepodge of your life—the things that have happened to you and the things you've dreamed of happening. They're the raw material of both. Then, if you're a writer, like me, you try less to impose a shape on the hodgepodge than to see what shape emerges from it. You try to sense in what direction the hodgepodge of your life is moving. You listen to it. You avoid forcing your characters to march too steadily to the drumbeat of your artistic purpose. You leave some measure of real freedom for your characters to be themselves. And if minor characters show an inclination to become major characters, as they're apt to do, you at least give them a shot at it, because in the world of fiction it may take many pages before you find out who the major characters really are, just as in the real world it may take you many years to find out that the stranger you talked to once for half an hour in the railway station may have done more to point you to where your true homeland lies than your priest or your best friend or even your psychiatrist.

Of course anybody who writes books uses as much craft as there is at hand. I certainly do that myself. I figure out what scenes to put in and—almost as hard—what scenes to leave out. I decide when to use dialogue and spend hours trying to make it sound like human beings talking to each other instead of like me talking to myself. I labor to find the right tone of voice, the right style, ultimately the right word to tell my story in, which is the hardest part, I suppose, of writing—sentence after sentence, page after page, looking for the word that has freshness and color and life.

I try not to let my own voice be the dominant one. It's hard to do that. The limitation of the great stylists—Henry James, say, or Hemingway—is that you remember their voices long after you've forgotten the voices of any of the people they wrote about. In one of the Psalms, God says, "Be still and know that I am God." I've always taken that to be good literary advice, too. Be still the way Tolstoy is still, be still the way Anthony Trollope is still, so that your characters can become gods and speak for themselves and come alive in their own way.

In both faith and fiction you *fashion* out of the raw stuff of your experience. If you want to remain open to luck and grace, you *shape* that stuff, less to impose a shape on it than to discover what the shape is. And in both, you *feign*. Feigning is imagining—making visible images for invisible things. Fiction has no way of being "true," the way a photograph is true; at its best it can only feign truth, the way a good portrait does, arriving at an inward, invisible truth. It can be true to the experience of being alive in the world, and what you write obviously depends on which part of your experience you choose to write about.

The part that has always most interested me is illustrated by incidents like the three I told you about at the start: the moment that unaccountably brings tears to your eyes, that takes you by crazy surprise, that sends a shiver down your spine, that haunts you with what is just possibly a glimpse of something far beyond or deep within itself. That's the part of human experience I choose to write about in my fiction. It's the part I'm most concerned to feign—that is, to make images for. In that sense I can live with the label of "religious novelist."

In any other sense I consider it the kiss of death. I lean over backward not to preach or to propagandize in my novels. I don't dream up plots and characters to illustrate some homiletic message. God forbid! I'm not bent on driving home some theological point. I'm simply trying to conjure up stories in which people are touched with what may or may not be the presence of God in their lives, the way I believe we all are as surely as I believe that I'm standing at this lectern, though most of us might sooner be shot dead than use that kind of language to describe it. In my own experience the ways God appears in our lives are elusive and ambiguous always. There's always room for doubt—in order, perhaps, that there will always be room to breathe. There's so much in life that hides God and denies the very possibility of God that sometimes it's hard not to deny God altogether. Yet it's still possible to have faith, in spite of all those things. Faith is that "in spite of." That's the experience I'm trying to be true to—in the same way that other novelists are trying to be true to the experience of being, say, a woman, or being an infantryman in the Second World War, or being black, or being whatever.

For all those novelists there is nothing more crucial than honesty. If you're going to be a religious novelist (and I'm not urging anybody) you've got to be honest not just about the times that glimmer with God's presence but also about the times that are dark with His absence because, needless to say, you've had your dark times just like everybody else.

TERRIBLE THINGS HAPPEN, for instance, in the four novels I wrote about a character named Leo Bebb. Bebb's wife, Lucille, kills her own baby. And when Bebb tells her long afterward that she has been washed clean with the Blood of the Lamb, she says, "The only thing I've been washed in is the shit of the horse," and dies a suicide. Poor Brownie, another character, reeking of aftershave, decides that his rose-colored faith is as false as his teeth and loses his faith. Miriam Parr dies of cancer, wondering if she's "going someplace," as she puts it, or "just going out like a match."

The narrator of these four novels is a feckless young man named Antonio Parr, who starts out in the first book with no sense of commitment to anything or anybody, but who, through his relationship with Leo Bebb, gradually comes alive with at least the possibility of something like religious faith. He has learned to listen for God in the things that happen to him, just in case there happens to be a God to listen to. Maybe all he can hear, he says, quoting Andrew Marvell, is "time's wingèd chariot hurrying near." Or, if there's more to it than that, the most he can say of it constitutes the passage that ends the last of those four novels, where the narrator uses the Lone Ranger as an image for Christ and says:

> To be honest, I must say that on occasion I hear something else too—not the thundering of distant hooves, maybe, or "Hi-yo, Silver, away!" echoing across the lonely sage, but the faint chunk-chunk of my own moccasin heart, of the Tonto afoot in the dusk of me somewhere, who, not because he ought to but because he can't help himself, whispers "*kemo sabe*" every once in a while to what may or may not be only a silvery trick of the failing light.

So terrible things as well as wonderful things happen in those novels. But it's not so much that I have to cook them up in order to give a balanced view of the way life is. It's that they have a way of happening as much on their own in the fictional world as they do in the real world. If you're preaching from a pulpit or otherwise grinding an ax, you only let the things happen that you want to have happen. But insofar as fiction, like faith, is a journey not only forward in space and time but a journey inward, it's full of surprises, the way dreams are. Even the wonderful things, the things that religious writers in the propagandist sense would presumably orchestrate and control, tend at their best to come as a surprise, and that's what's most wonderful about them. Again, in the case of the Bebb books, for instance, I was well along into the first of them, *Lion Country*, before I came to the conviction that Bebb himself was a saint. I hadn't known that. It was a marvelous surprise.

Imagine setting out *consciously* to write a novel about a saint. Think about that. How could a writer avoid falling flat on his face? Nothing is harder to make real than holiness. Certainly nothing is harder to make appealing and attractive. The danger is that you start out with the idea that sainthood is something people achieve—that you get to be holy more or less the way you get to be an Eagle Scout. To create a saint from that point of view would be to end up with something on the order of Little Nell. The truth, of course, is that holiness is not a human quality at all, like virtue. Holiness is Godness, and as such it's not something that people do, but something that God does in them.

It's something God seems especially apt to do to people who aren't virtuous at all, at least not to start with. Think of Francis of Assisi, or Mary Magdalene. If you're too virtuous, the chances are you think you're a saint already under your own steam, and therefore the real thing can't happen to you.

Leo Bebb, God knows, was not an Eagle Scout. He ran a religious diploma mill and ordained people through the mail for a fee. He did five years in the pen on a charge of indecent exposure involving children. He had a child with the wife of his twin brother. But he was a risk-taker. He was as round and fat and full of bounce as a rubber ball. He was without pretense. He was good company. Above all, he was extraordinarily alive—so much so for me, anyway, that when I was writing about him it was like a love affair. I couldn't wait to get to my study every morning. That's when I began not only to see that he was a saint but to see what a saint is.

A saint is a life-giver. I hadn't known that. A saint is a human being with the same hang-ups and dark secrets and abysses as the rest of us. But if a saint touches your life, you come alive in a new way. Even aimless, involuted Antonio Parr came more alive through knowing Bebb, though at first he was out to expose him as a fake. So did the theosophist Gertrude Conover, Bebb's blue-haired octogenarian paramour. More extraordinary yet, *I* came more alive. I'm a bookish, private sort of man, not given to . . . making a fool of myself, but in my old age I find myself doing and saying all sorts of outrageous things which, before Bebb came into my life and into my fiction, I would never have even considered. I didn't think Bebb up at all, the way he finally emerged as a character; sometimes I wonder if he was the one who thought *me* up. I had an entirely different character in mind when I started. But in his tight-fitting raincoat and Tyrolean hat Bebb simply turned out to be the person he was in my journey of writing those books. I didn't expect him. I didn't deserve him. He came making no conditions; there were no strings attached. He was a gift to me.

AND THAT'S ALSO (I want to be theological for a moment) what grace is. Grace is a gift, totally free. Grace is God in his givenness. "Inspiration" is the word that writers are apt to use for it—inspiration as a breathing into. In fiction, as in faith, something from outside ourselves is breathed into us if we're lucky and if we're open enough to inhale it. I think writers of religious fiction have to stay open in that way. They've got to play their hunches more and take risks more. They shouldn't try to keep too tight a rein on what they're doing. They should be willing to be less professional and less literary and to be more eccentric and more antic and more disheveled. Less like John Updike, let's say, or Walker Percy—very literary, very good—and more like Kurt Vonnegut or Peter De Vries or G. K. Chesterton.

In the stories of Flannery O'Connor, for instance, I have the feeling of the author herself being caught off guard by a flash of insight here, a stab of feeling there. She's making discoveries about holy things, about human things, in a way that she herself says would not have been possible if she had known too well where she was going and how she was going to get there. And as her readers we share in the freshness and the wonder of her surprise.

That greatest of all novels, *The Brothers Karamazov*, is a classic example of what I'm talking about—that great seething bouillabaisse of a book. It's digressive and sprawling, many too many characters in it, much too long, and yet it's a book which, just because Dostoyevsky leaves room in it for whatever comes up to enter, is entered here and there by maybe nothing less than the Holy Spirit itself, thereby becoming, as far as I'm concerned, what a religious novel at its best can be—that is, a novel less *about* the religious experience than a novel the reading of which *is* a religious experience: of God, both in his subterranean presence and in his appalling absence.

Is it the Holy Spirit? Is it the muse? Is it just a lucky break when these things happen in a story or in a life? Who dares say either way without crossing his fingers? But as in the journey of faith, it's possible every once in a while to be better than you are. Saint Paul says, "Do you not know that God's spirit dwells in you?" In the journey of fiction-making it's possible to write more than you know.

Bebb was a saint—a kind of saint, anyway—and when I finally finished with him, or he with me, I found it was very hard to write a novel about anybody who wasn't a saint. I tried to write a novel about a fifteenth-century alchemist. I tried to write a novel about a twentieth-century woman novelist. I tried to write a novel about a dishwasher in a restaurant in Manchester, Vermont. I tried to write one about an old lady in a nursing home. But one by one they all failed to come to life for me. They were all in their own way too much like me, I suppose, and after so many years I've become tired of me. And too many other authors were writing novels about people like that, many of them better than I could do it, so why add to the number? Then I realized that the reason why none of them worked for me was that, after Bebb, only saints really interested me as a writer, and I've spent my life since then writing about them. There's so much life in them. They're so in touch with, so transparent to, the mystery of things that you never know what to expect from them. Anything is possible for a saint. They won't stay put or be led around by the nose, no matter how you try.

THEN ONE DAY, entirely by accident, or by grace, or by luck, I came across a historical saint, named Godric, whom I'd never heard of before, who was born in England in 1065 and died there in 1170. If, like me, you don't happen to be a saint yourself, I don't know how you could possibly write about one without being given something from somewhere. That's especially true if you try, as I did, to make the saint himself your narrator, so that you have his whole interior life on your hands as well as his career. Add to that, Godric was a man who was born close to a thousand years ago. He lived in a different world, spoke a different language and saw things in a different way.

I did some research, needless to say—not the exhaustive kind that a real historical novelist does, because it wasn't primarily the history I was interested in, but Godric himself. Still, I did read enough to give myself a rough idea of what was going on in Europe at the time, especially in England. Largely through the ineffable *Dictionary of National Biography* I found out what I could about the historical figures who played some part in Godric's life, such as Abbot Ailred of Rievaulx Abbey and Ranulf Flambard, the bishop of Durham and former chancellor to William II. I tried, with very little success, to find out what Rome and Jerusalem looked like when Godric made his pilgrimages there. And I dug a little into the First Crusade because Godric was apparently involved with it briefly.

The principal source on Godric himself is a biography by someone who knew him, a monk known as Reginald of Durham, who also figures as a character in my novel. His book has never to this day been translated from medieval Latin into English. And in that connection something remarkable happened, comparable to my discovery of the tie clip with my initials on it. My own Latin came to an end when I was thirteen years old at the Lawrenceville School and had such a miserable time with Caesar's *Commentaries* that I gave it up forever. So the best I could do with this book in medieval Latin was to look up some promising items in the (happily) English index and then try to get the gist of the passages with the help of a dictionary. Just as I was getting started, struggling with this monstrous book, one of my daughters, who was off at boarding school, phoned to ask if she could bring some friends home for the weekend. And one of the friends turned out to be the chairman of the school's classics department—the only man, I suspect, within a radius of a million miles who could have done the job—and we sat together for a couple of hours two evenings in a row and he gave me sight translations of the passages I was after.

But I'm talking about something even odder than that, and a lot more precious. I'm talking about how, by something like grace, you're given every once in a while to be better than you are and to write more than you know. Not because of the research I did but in spite of it, Godric came alive for me. That's what I was given: the way he thought, the way he spoke, the humanness of him, the holiness of him. I don't think any writer can do that just by taking thought and effort and using the customary tools of the craft. Something else has to happen—something more mysterious. Godric not only came alive for me; he came speaking words that had a life and a twist to them that I can't feel entirely responsible for. I don't want to make it sound spookier than it was—I was the writer who wrote Godric's words; I dredged them up out of some sub-basement of who I am. But the words that I found were much more like him than they were like me, and without him—whatever I mean by that—I feel certain that I never could have found them or written them.

Year after year, in the north of England, which I went to see again last year to remind myself of it, that old hermit Godric used to chasten his flesh in all seasons by bathing in the river Wear, which runs by Durham, at a place called Finchale. When he got too feeble to do that, to stagger down over the rocks and immerse his old carcass in that frigid water, he had a servant dig a hole in the chapel he had built for the Virgin Mary with his own hands out of wood (this is all from Reginald's life), and the servant would fill that hole up with water from the river so that Godric could still bathe in it. Here's a passage from my novel in which Godric describes what it was like to bathe first in the river itself and later in the little pool in the chapel:

> First there's the fiery sting of cold that almost stops my breath, the aching torment in my limbs. I think I may go mad, my wits so outraged that they seek to flee my skull like rats [on] a ship that's going down. I puff. I gasp. Then inch by inch a blessed numbness comes. I have no legs, no arms. My very heart grows still. These floating hands are not my hands. This ancient flesh I wear is rags for all I feel of it.
>
> "Praise, praise!" I croak. Praise God for all that's holy, cold and dark. Praise him for all we lose, for all the river of the years bears off. Praise him for stillness in the wake of pain. Praise him for

emptiness. And as you race to spill into the sea, praise him yourself, old Wear. Praise him for dying and the peace of death.

In the little church I built of wood for Mary, I hollowed out a place for him. Perkin brings him by the pail and pours him in. Now that I can hardly walk, I crawl to meet him there. He takes me in his chilly lap to wash me of my sins. Or I kneel down beside him till within his depths I see a star.

Sometimes this star is still. Sometimes she dances. She is Mary's star. Within that little pool of Wear she winks at me. I wink at her. The secret that we share I cannot tell in full. But this much I will tell. What's lost is nothing to what's found, and all the death that ever was, set next to life, would scarcely fill a cup.

Feigning is part of it. Imagining; image-making; reaching deep. But it feels like more than that, is what I'm trying to say. Godric told me things I didn't know. He revealed something of himself to me and something of the distant past. He also revealed something of myself to me and something of the not-so-distant future. Like Godric I'll grow old and I'll die. I think it was through his eyes that I first saw beyond the inevitability of that to the mercy of it. "All's lost. All's found." I have faith that that is true, or someday will turn out to be true, but on the old saint's lips the words have a ring of certitude and benediction from which I draw courage, as I know I couldn't draw courage from words merely of my own.

Is that why we write, year after year, people like me—to keep our courage up? Are novels like mine a kind of whistling in the dark? I think so. To whistle in the dark is more than just to try to convince yourself that dark is not all there is. It's also to *remind* yourself that dark is not all there is, or the end of all there is, because even in the dark there is hope. Even in the dark you have the power to whistle. And sometimes that seems more than just your own power because it's powerful enough to hold the dark back a little. The tunes you whistle in the dark are the images you make of that hope, that power. They are the books you write.

And in the same way, faith could also be called a kind of whistling in the dark. The living out of faith. The writing out of fiction. In both, you shape and you fashion and you feign. And maybe, finally, what the two have most richly in common is that they are a way of paying attention. Page by page, chapter by chapter, the story unfolds. Day by day, year by year, your own story unfolds—your life story. Things happen. People come and people go. The scene shifts. Time runs by. Time runs out.

Maybe it's all utterly meaningless. Maybe it's all unutterably meaningful. If you want to know which, pay attention to what it means to be truly human in a world that half the time we're in love with and half the time scares the hell out of us. Any fiction that helps us pay attention to that is religious fiction. The unexpected sound of your name on somebody's lips. The good dream. The strange coincidence. The moment that brings tears to your eyes. The person who brings life to your life. Even the smallest events hold the greatest clues. If it's God we're looking for, as I suspect we all are, maybe the reason we haven't found Him is that we're not looking very hard.

So pay attention. As a summation of all that I've ever had to say as a writer I'd settle for that. And as a talisman or motto for that journey in search of a homeland, which is what faith is, I'd settle for that, too.

John L'Heureux

FAITH

The Expert on God

From the start faith had been a problem for him, and his recent ordination had changed almost nothing. His doubts were simply more appropriate to the priesthood now. That was the only difference.

As a child of ten he was saying his evening prayers when it suddenly struck him that Catholics believed in three gods, God the Father, God the Son, and God the Holy Ghost. He blushed and covered his face. What if the kids at school found out? They were Protestants, and therefore wrong, but at least they had only one God. Instantly it came to him that there were three *Persons* in one God. It was a mystery. He was very embarrassed but very relieved, and he actually looked around to see if anyone had heard his thoughts, and for the rest of his life it remained for him a moment of great shame. At eighteen, when he entered the Jesuits, he got up his courage and told this story to his confessor, who laughed. Matters of faith, he decided then, were better kept secret.

There were other doubts. He doubted Christ's presence in the Eucharist. He prayed for faith, and some kind of faith came to him, because he left off doubting about the Eucharist and moved on to doubt other matters: the virginity of Mary, the divinity of Christ, and then later the humanity of Christ. At one time or another, he doubted every article of belief, but only for a while, and only one at a time. Faith demanded a different response to each mystery, he discovered, but doubt was always the same. The initial onslaught of doubt lasted for only a moment, a quick and breathtaking conviction that none of it was true, and then that conviction itself surrendered to doubt, leaving an awful lingering unspeakable ache.

In the end he doubted the love of God, and that doubt did not pass.

He was a popular priest but he had no friends. He kept other Jesuits at a distance, he forced them away. He had no time for the intimacies of his own kind, caught up as he was in his assault on God. He prayed for faith. And when that did not come, he prayed for hope. And when that did not come, he went on anyway, teaching, preaching, saying Mass at the odd parish whenever he was asked. That is how things stood with him on the day of the accident.

It was Christmas Day, not because Christmas is symbolic, but because that is when it happened. Snow had fallen for nearly a week, and then on Christmas Eve there had been hail and then rain and then a sudden freeze. The streets were ready.

He had said Mass at our Lady of Victories and was driving back to the Jesuit house. It was almost noon and the sun was high. "It doesn't matter," he said. The air was clear and the day was bright after all that snow, and as he drove through the vast open countryside, he marveled again at the absence of God. "It doesn't matter anymore."

He had very nearly achieved a kind of trance, staring at the sun on the ice, trying to obliterate all thought. Suddenly, off to the side of the road, he saw a dark blue car turned half on its side and three boys huddled near it, looking at him as if he might be bringing help. He braked quickly, skidded in a half-turn, and came to a stop. It was then that he noticed the tiny red sports car in the field on the opposite side of the road. It was crumpled nearly in two. The priest looked at the boys, but they only looked back, stunned. Finally one of them pointed to the red sports car.

He scrabbled through the glove compartment until he found the little vial of holy oils. He sprinted toward the car, following the wild track it had made as it spun through the snow, and when he got to it, he was not surprised to see the front end was completely demolished. He stooped and looked through the shattered window. The driver had been thrown to the side; the dashboard, crumpled back into the car, had pinned him, head down, in the passenger seat. The door hung on a single hinge, open a few inches but not wide enough for the priest to get in. The door would not give and he could not force it to open wider. He looked around a moment for help and saw that of course there was none; the boys huddling together across the street were too stupefied to help—or maybe they were injured, for all he knew.

He put the vial of oils in his pocket and jogged rapidly around the car. There was no way in. Somebody was inside, dying perhaps, and though he was only a few inches away, he could not reach him. It was maddening. He struck the car with his fist and sobbed suddenly in anger and frustration. Desperate then, he braced his back against the side of the car, pushing outward on the broken door and twisting, half crazy, until the hinge gave way. He squeezed himself into the car behind the driver's seat. He could hear a kind of gurgling sound from the man trapped beneath the dashboard. He edged across until he was behind the passenger seat and, with what strength he could muster, he pulled back on it until it snapped and broke loose. He climbed onto it so that he was behind the body. He squatted, doubled up, hunched over, scarcely able to breathe, but at last he got his arms around the body and eased it free of the dashboard.

It was a boy, in his new car, and he was still alive, or nearly. He made a sound that might have been a sigh or a groan. Blood trickled from his mouth. Still he did not die.

The priest held him in his arms. Crushed himself, he nonetheless managed to get the oils from his pocket and to wet his thumb with them and to place his thumb on the boy's bloody forehead, saying "I absolve you from all your sins. In the name of the Father and of the Son and of the Holy Ghost. Amen." Then he was silent.

There was no sound from outside the car, no ambulance wail, no curious viewers. They were in the middle of nowhere, he and this dying boy he held in his arms. He had touched the boy with the holy oils and he had offered him absolution for his sins, and something should have happened by now. Someone should have come to help. The boy should have died. Something. But there was silence only, and the boy's harsh, half-choked breathing.

He began to pray, aloud, which struck him as foolish: to be holding a dying boy in his arms and reciting rote prayers about our father in heaven, about holy Mary, mother of God. What could he do? What could he say at such a moment? What would God do at such a moment, if there were a God? "Well, do it," he said aloud, and heard the fury in his voice. "Say something." But there was silence from heaven.

His doubts became certainty and he said, "It doesn't matter," but it did matter and he knew it. What could anyone say to this crushed, dying thing, he wondered. What would God say if he cared as much as I?

He shook with an involuntary sob then, and as he did, the boy shuddered in agony and choked on the blood that had begun to pour from his mouth. The priest could see death beginning to ease across the boy's face. And still he could say nothing.

The boy turned—some dying reflex—and his head tilted in the priest's arms, trusting, like a lover. And at once the priest, faithless, unrepentant, gave up his prayers and bent to him and whispered, fierce and burning, "I love you," and continued till there was no breath. "I love you, I love you, I love you."

Gabriel García Márquez

FAITH

The Saint

I SAW MARGARITO DUARTE after twenty-two years on one of the narrow secret streets in Trastevere, and at first I had trouble recognizing him, because he spoke halting Spanish and had the appearance of an old Roman. His hair was white and thin, and there was nothing left of the Andean intellectual's solemn manner and funereal clothes with which he had first come to Rome, but in the course of our conversation I began, little by little, to recover him from the treachery of his years and see him again as he had been: secretive, unpredictable, and as tenacious as a stonecutter. Before the second cup of coffee in one of our bars from the old days, I dared to ask the question that was gnawing inside me.

"What happened with the Saint?"

"The Saint is there," he answered. "Waiting."

Only the tenor Rafael Ribero Silva and I could understand the enormous human weight of his reply. We knew his drama so well that for years I thought Margarito Duarte was the character in search of an author that we novelists wait for all our lives, and if I never allowed him to find me it was because the end of his story seemed unimaginable.

He had come to Rome during that radiant spring when Pius XII suffered from an attack of hiccups that neither the good nor the evil arts of physicians and wizards could cure. It was his first time away from Tolima, his village high in the Colombian Andes—a fact that was obvious even in the way he slept. He presented himself one morning at our consulate carrying the polished pine box the shape and size of a cello case, and he explained the surprising reason for his trip to the consul, who then telephoned his countryman, the tenor Rafael Ribero Silva, asking that he find him a room at the *pensione* where we both lived. That is how I met him.

Margarito Duarte had not gone beyond primary school, but his vocation for letters had permitted him a broader education through the impassioned reading of everything in print he could lay his hands on. At the age of eighteen, when he was village clerk, he married a beautiful girl who died not long afterward when she gave birth to their first child, a daughter. Even more beautiful than her mother, she died of an essential fever at the age of seven. But the real story of Margarito Duarte began six months before his arrival in Rome, when the construction of a dam required that the cemetery in his village be moved. Margarito, like all the other residents of the region, disinterred the bones of his dead to carry them to the new cemetery. His wife was dust. But in the grave next to hers, the girl was still intact after eleven years. In fact, when they pried the lid off the coffin, they could smell the scent of the fresh-cut roses with which she had been buried. Most astonishing of all, however, was that her body had no weight.

Hundreds of curiosity-seekers, attracted by the resounding news of the miracle, poured into the village. There was no doubt about it: The incorruptibility of the body was an unequivocal sign of sainthood, and even the bishop of the diocese agreed that such a prodigy should be submitted to the judgment of the Vatican. And therefore they took up a public collection so that Margarito Duarte could travel to Rome to do battle for the cause that no longer was his alone or limited to the narrow confines of his village, but had become a national issue.

As he told us his story in the *pensione* in the quiet Parioli district, Margarito Duarte removed the padlock and raised the lid of the beautiful trunk. That was how the tenor Ribero Silva and I participated in the miracle. She did not resemble the kind of withered mummy seen in so many museums of the world, but a little girl dressed as a bride who was still sleeping after a long stay underground. Her skin was smooth and warm, and her open eyes were clear and created the unbearable impression that they were looking at us from death. The satin and artificial orange blossoms of her crown had not withstood the rigors of time as well as her skin, but the roses that had been placed in her hands were still alive. And it was in fact true that the weight of the pine case did not change when we removed the body.

Margarito Duarte began his negotiations the day following his arrival, at first with diplomatic assistance that was more compassionate than efficient, and then with every strategy he could think of to circumvent the countless barriers set up by the Vatican. He was always very reserved about the measures he was taking, but we knew they were numerous and to no avail. He communicated with all the religious congregations and humanitarian foundations he could find, and they listened to him with attention but no surprise and promised immediate steps that were never taken. The truth is that it was not the most propitious time. Everything having to do with the Holy See had been postponed until the Pope overcame the attack of hiccuping that proved resistant not only to the most refined techniques of academic medicine, but to every kind of magic remedy sent to him from all over the world.

At last, in the month of July, Pius XII recovered and left for his summer vacation in Castel Gandolfo. Margarito took the Saint to the first weekly audience, hoping he could show her to the Pope, who appeared in the inner courtyard on a balcony so low that Margarito could see his burnished fingernails and smell his lavender scent. He did not circulate among the tourists who came from every nation to see him, as Margarito had anticipated, but repeated the same statement in six languages and concluded with a general blessing.

After so many delays, Margarito decided to take matters into his own hands, and he delivered a letter almost sixty pages long to the Secretariat of State but received no reply. He had foreseen this, for the functionary who accepted his handwritten letter with all due formality did not deign to give more than an official glance at the dead girl, and the clerks passing by looked at her with no interest at all. One of them told him that in the previous year they had received more than eight hundred letters requesting sainthood for intact corpses in various places around the globe. At last Margarito requested that the weightlessness of the body be verified. The functionary verified it but refused to admit it.

"It must be a case of collective suggestion," he said.

In his few free hours, and on the dry Sundays of summer, Margarito remained in his room, devouring any book that seemed relevant to his cause. At the end of each month, on his own initiative, he wrote a detailed calculation of his expenses in a composition book, using the exquisite calligraphy of a senior clerk to provide the contributors from his village with strict and up-to-date accounts. Before the year was out he knew the labyrinths of Rome as if he had been born there, spoke a fluent Italian as laconic as his Andean Spanish, and knew as much as anyone about the process of canonization. But much more time passed before he changed his funereal dress, the vest and magistrate's hat which in the Rome of that time were typical of certain secret societies with unconfessable aims. He went out very early with the case that held the Saint, and sometimes he returned late at night, exhausted and sad but always with a spark of light that filled him with new courage for the next day.

"Saints live in their own time," he would say.

It was my first visit to Rome, where I was studying at the Experimental Film Center, and I lived his calvary with unforgettable intensity. Our *pensione* was in reality a modern apartment a few steps from the Villa Borghese. The owner occupied two rooms and rented the other four to foreign students. We called her Bella Maria, and in the ripeness of her autumn she was good-looking and temperamental and always faithful to the sacred rule that each man is absolute king of his own room. The one who really bore the burden of daily life was her older sister, Aunt Antonietta, an angel without wings who worked for her hour after hour during the day, moving through the apartment with her pail and brush, polishing the marble floor beyond the realm of the possible. It was she who taught us to eat the little songbirds that her husband, Bartolino, caught—a bad habit left over from the war—and who, in the end, took Margarito to live in her house when he could no longer afford Bella Maria's prices.

Nothing was less suited to Margarito's nature than that house without law. Each hour had some surprise in store for us, even the dawn, when we were awakened by the fearsome roar of the lion in the Villa Borghese zoo. The tenor Ribero Silva had earned this privilege: the Romans did not resent his early-morning practice sessions. He would get up at six, take his medicinal bath of icy water, arrange his Mephistophelean beard and eyebrows, and only when he was ready, and wearing his tartan bathrobe, Chinese silk scarf, and personal cologne, give himself over, body and soul, to his vocal exercises. He would throw open the window in his room, even when the wintry stars were still in the sky, and warm up with progressive phrasings of great love arias until he was singing at full voice. The daily expectation was that when he sang his *do* at top volume, the Villa Borghese lion would answer him with an earth-shaking roar.

"You are the reincarnation of Saint Mark, *figlio mio*," Aunt Antonietta would exclaim in true amazement. "Only he could talk to lions."

One morning it was not the lion who replied. The tenor began the love duet from *Othello*—"*Già nella notte densa s'estingue ogni clamor*"—and from the bottom of the courtyard we heard the answer, in a beautiful soprano voice. The tenor continued, and the two voices sang the complete selection to the delight of all the neighbors, who opened the windows to sanctify their houses with the torrent of that irresistible love.

The tenor almost fainted when he learned that his invisible Desdemona was no less a personage than the great Maria Caniglia.

I have the impression that this episode gave Margarito Duarte a valid reason for joining in the life of the house. From that time on he sat with the rest of us at the common table and not, as he had done at first, in the kitchen, where Aunt Antonietta indulged him almost every day with her masterly songbird stew. When the meal was over, Bella Maria would read the daily papers aloud to teach us Italian phonetics, and comment on the news with an arbitrariness and wit that brought joy to our lives. One day, with regard to the Saint, she told us that in the city of Palermo there was an enormous museum that held the incorruptible corpses of men, women, and children, and even several bishops, who had all been disinterred from the same Capuchin cemetery. The news so disturbed Margarito that he did not have a moment's peace until we went to Palermo. But a passing glance at the oppressive galleries of inglorious mummies was all he needed to make a consolatory judgment.

"These are not the same," he said. "You can tell right away they're dead."

After lunch Rome would succumb to its August stupor. The afternoon sun remained immobile in the middle of the sky, and in the two-o'clock silence one heard nothing but water, which is the natural voice of Rome. But at about seven the windows were thrown open to summon the cool air that began to circulate, and a jubilant crowd took to the streets with no other purpose than to live, in the midst of backfiring motorcycles, the shouts of melon vendors, and love songs among the flowers on the terraces.

The tenor and I did not take a siesta. We would ride on his Vespa, he driving and I sitting behind, and bring ices and chocolates to the little summer whores who fluttered under the centuries-old laurels in the Villa Borghese and watched for sleepless tourists in the bright sun. They were beautiful, poor, and affectionate, like most Italian women in those days, and they dressed in blue organdy, pink poplin, green linen, and protected themselves from the sun with parasols damaged by storms of bullets during the recent war. It was a human pleasure to be with them, because they ignored the rules of their trade and allowed themselves the luxury of losing a good client in order to have coffee and conversation with us in the bar on the corner, or take carriage rides around the paths in the park, or fill us with pity for the deposed monarchs and their tragic mistresses who rode horseback at dusk along the *galoppatoio*. More than once we served as their interpreters with some foreigner gone astray.

They were not the reason we took Margarito Duarte to the Villa Borghese: We wanted him to see the lion. He lived uncaged on a small desert island in the middle of a deep moat, and as soon as he caught sight of us on the far shore he began to roar with an agitation that astonished his keeper. The visitors to the park gathered around in surprise. The tenor tried to identify himself with his full-voiced morning *do*, but the lion paid him no attention. He seemed to roar at all of us without distinction, yet the keeper knew right away that he roared only for Margarito. It was true: Wherever he moved the lion moved, and as soon as he was out of sight the lion stopped roaring. The keeper, who held a doctorate in classical literature from the University of Siena, thought that Margarito had been with other lions that day and was carrying their scent. Aside from that reasoning, which was invalid, he could think of no other explanation.

"In any event," he said, "they are roars of compassion, not battle."

And yet what most affected the tenor Ribero Silva was not that supernatural episode, but Margarito's confusion when they stopped to talk with the girls in the park. He remarked on it at the table, and we all agreed—some in order to make mischief and others because they were sympathetic—that it would be a good idea to help Margarito resolve his loneliness. Moved by our tender hearts, Bella Maria pressed her hands, covered by rings with imitation stones, against her bosom worthy of a doting biblical matriarch.

"I would do it for charity's sake," she said, "except that I never could abide men who wear vests."

That was how the tenor rode his Vespa to the Villa Borghese at two in the afternoon and returned with the little butterfly he thought best able to give Margarito Duarte an hour of good company. He had her undress in his bedroom, bathed her with scented soap, dried her, perfumed her with his personal cologne, and dusted her entire body with his camphorated aftershave talc. And then he paid her for the time they had already spent, plus another hour, and told her step by step what she had to do.

The naked beauty tiptoed through the shadowy house, like a siesta dream, gave two gentle little taps at the rear bedroom door, and Margarito Duarte appeared, barefoot and shirtless.

"*Buona sera, giovanotto,*" she said, with the voice and manners of a schoolgirl. "*Mi manda il tenore.*"

Margarito absorbed the shock with great dignity. He opened the door wide to let her in, and she lay down on the bed while he rushed to put on his shirt and shoes to receive her with all due respect. Then he sat beside her on a chair and began the conversation. The bewildered girl told him to hurry because they only had an hour. He did not seem to understand.

The girl said later that in any event she would have spent all the time he wanted and not charged him a cent, because there could not be a better-behaved man anywhere in the world. Not knowing what to do in the meantime, she glanced around the room and saw the wooden case near the fireplace. She asked if it was a saxophone. Margarito did not answer, but opened the blind to let in a little light, carried the case to the bed, and raised the lid. The girl tried to say something, but her jaw was hanging open. Or as she told us later: "*Mi si gelò il culo.*" She fled in utter terror, but lost her way in the hall and ran into Aunt Antonietta, who was going to my room to replace a light bulb. They were both so frightened that the girl did not dare leave the tenor's room until very late that night.

Aunt Antonietta never learned what happened. She came into my room in such fear that she could not turn the bulb in the lamp because her hands were shaking. I asked her what was wrong. "There are ghosts in this house," she said. "And now in broad daylight." She told me with great conviction that during the war a German officer had cut the throat of his mistress in the room occupied by the tenor. As Aunt Antonietta went about her work, she often saw the ghost of the beautiful victim making her way along the corridors.

"I've just seen her walking naked down the hall," she said. "She was identical."

The city resumed its autumn routine. The flowering terraces of summer closed down with the first winds, and the tenor and I returned to our old haunts in Trastevere, where we ate supper with the vocal students of Count Carlo Calcagni, and with some of my classmates from the film school, among whom the most faithful was Lakis, an intelligent, amiable Greek whose soporific discourses on social injustice were his only fault. It was our good fortune that the tenors and sopranos almost always drowned him out with operatic selections that they sang at full volume, but which did not bother anyone, even after midnight. On the contrary, some late-night passersby would join in the chorus, and neighbors opened their windows to applaud.

One night, while we were singing, Margarito tiptoed in so as not to interrupt us. He was carrying the pine case that he had not had time to leave at the *pensione* after showing the Saint to the parish priest at San Giovanni in Laterano, whose influence with the Holy Congregation of the Rite was common knowledge. From the corner of my eye I caught a glimpse of him putting it under the isolated table where he sat until we finished singing. As always, just after midnight, when the trattoria began to empty, we would push several tables together and sit in one group—those who sang, those of us who talked about movies, and all our friends. And among them Margarito Duarte, who was already known there as the silent, melancholy Colombian whose life was a mystery. Lakis was intrigued and asked him if he played the cello. I was caught off guard by what seemed to me an indiscretion too difficult to handle. The tenor was just as uncomfortable and could not save the situation. Margarito was the only one who responded to the question with absolute naturalness.

"It's not a cello," he said. "It's the Saint."

He placed the case on the table, opened the padlock, and raised the lid. A gust of stupefaction shook the restaurant. The other customers, the waiters, even the people in the kitchen with their bloodstained aprons, gathered in astonishment to see the miracle. Some crossed themselves. One of the cooks, overcome by a feverish trembling, fell to her knees with clasped hands and prayed in silence.

And yet when the initial commotion was over, we became involved in a shouting argument about the lack of saintliness in our day. Lakis, of course, was the most radical. The only clear idea at the end of it was that he wanted to make a critical movie about the Saint.

"I'm sure," he said, "that old Cesare would never let this subject get away."

He was referring to Cesare Zavattini, who taught us plot development and screenwriting. He was one of the great figures in the history of film, and the only one who maintained a personal relationship with us outside class. He tried to teach us not only the craft but a different way of looking at life. He was a machine for inventing plots. They poured out of him, almost against his will, and with such speed that he always needed someone to help catch them in mid-flight as he thought them up aloud. His enthusiasm would flag only when he had completed them. "Too bad they have to be filmed," he would say. For he thought that on the screen they would lose much of their original magic. He kept his ideas on cards arranged by subject and pinned to the walls, and he had so many they filled an entire room in his house.

The following Saturday we took Margarito Duarte to see him. Zavattini was so greedy for life that we found him at the door of his house on the Via di Sant'Angela Merici, burning with interest in the idea we had described to him on the telephone. He did not even greet us with his customary amiability, but led Margarito to a table he had prepared, and opened the case himself. Then something happened that we never could have imagined. Instead of going wild, as we expected, he suffered a kind of mental paralysis.

"*Ammazza!*" he whispered in fear.

He looked at the Saint in silence for two or three minutes, closed the case himself, and without saying a word led Margarito to the door as if he were a child taking his first steps. He said good-bye with a few pats on his shoulder. “Thank you, my son, thank you very much,” he said. “And may God be with you in your struggle.” When he closed the door he turned toward us and gave his verdict.

"It’s no good for the movies,” he said. “Nobody would believe it.”

That surprising lesson rode with us on the streetcar we took home. If he said it, it had to be true: The story was no good. Yet Bella Maria met us at the *pensione* with the urgent message that Zavattini was expecting us that same night, but without Margarito.

We found the maestro in one of his stellar moments. Lakis had brought along two or three classmates, but he did not even seem to see them when he opened the door.

“I have it,” he shouted. “The picture will be a sensation if Margarito performs a miracle and resurrects the girl.”

“In the picture or in life?” I asked.

He suppressed his annoyance. “Don’t be stupid,” he said. But then we saw in his eyes the flash of an irresistible idea. “What if he could resurrect her in real life?” he mused, and added in all seriousness:

“He ought to try.”

It was no more than a passing temptation, and then he took up the thread again. He began to pace every room, like a happy lunatic, waving his hands and reciting the film in great shouts. We listened to him, dazzled, and it seemed we could see the images, like flocks of phosphorescent birds that he set loose for their mad flight through the house.

“One night,” he said, “after something like twenty popes who refused to receive him have died, Margarito grown old and tired goes into his house, opens the case, caresses the face of the little dead girl, and says with all the tenderness in the world: ‘For love of your father, my child, arise and walk.’”

He looked at all of us and finished with a triumphant gesture:

“And she does!”

He was waiting for something from us. But we were so befuddled we could not think of a thing to say. Except Lakis the Greek, who raised his hand, as if he were in school, to ask permission to speak.

"My problem is that I don't believe it," he said, and to our surprise he was speaking to Zavattini: "Excuse me, Maestro, but I don't believe it."

Then it was Zavattini's turn to be astonished.

"And why not?"

"How do I know?" said Lakis in anguish. "But it's impossible."

"*Ammazza!*" the maestro thundered in a voice that must have been heard throughout the entire neighborhood. "That's what I can't stand about Stalinists: They don't believe in reality."

For the next fifteen years, as he himself told me, Margarito carried the Saint to Castel Gandolfo in the event an opportunity arose for displaying her. At an audience for some two hundred pilgrims from Latin America, he managed to tell his story, amid shoves and pokes, to the benevolent John XXIII. But he could not show him the girl because, as a precaution against assassination attempts, he had been obliged to leave her at the entrance along with the knapsacks of the other pilgrims. The Pope listened with as much attention as he could in the crowd, and gave him an encouraging pat on the cheek.

"*Bravo, figlio mio,*" he said. "God will reward your perseverance."

But it was during the fleeting reign of the smiling Albino Luciani that Margarito really felt on the verge of fulfilling his dream. One of the Pope's relatives, impressed by Margarito's story, promised to intervene. No one paid him much attention. But two days later, as they were having lunch at the *pensione*, someone telephoned with a simple, rapid message for Margarito: He should not leave Rome, because sometime before Thursday he would be summoned to the Vatican for a private audience.

No one ever found out whether it was a joke. Margarito did not think so and stayed on the alert. He did not leave the house. If he had to go to the bathroom he announced: "I'm going to the bathroom." Bella Maria, still witty in the dawn of her old age, laughed her free woman's laugh.

"We know, Margarito," she shouted, "just in case the Pope calls."

Early one morning the following week Margarito almost collapsed when he saw the headline in the newspaper slipped under the door: "*Morto il Papa.*" For a moment he was sustained by the illusion that it was an old paper delivered by mistake, since it was not easy to believe that a pope would die every month. But it was true: The smiling Albino Luciani, elected thirty-three days earlier, had died in his sleep.

I returned to Rome twenty-two years after I first met Margarito Duarte, and perhaps I would not have thought about him at all if we had not run into each other by accident. I was too depressed by the ruinous weather to think about anybody. An imbecilic drizzle like warm soup never stopped falling, the diamond light of another time had turned muddy, and the places that had once been mine and sustained my memories were strange to me now. The building where the *pensione* was located had not changed, but nobody knew anything about Bella Maria. No one answered at the six different telephone numbers that the tenor Ribero Silva had sent me over the years. At lunch with new movie people, I evoked the memory of my teacher, and a sudden silence fluttered over the table for a moment until someone dared to say:

"*Zavattini? Mai sentito.*"

That was true: No one had heard of him. The trees in the Villa Borghese were disheveled in the rain, the *galoppatoio* of the sorrowful princesses had been devoured by weeds without flowers, and the beautiful girls of long ago had been replaced by athletic androgynes cross-dressed in flashy clothes. Among all the extinct fauna, the only survivor was the old lion, who suffered from mange and a head cold on his island surrounded by dried waters. No one sang or died of love in the plastic trattorias on the Piazza di Spagna. For the Rome of our memory was by now another ancient Rome within the ancient Rome of the Caesars. Then a voice that might have come from the beyond stopped me cold on a narrow street in Trastevere:

"Hello, Poet."

It was he, old and tired. Four popes had died, eternal Rome was showing the first signs of decrepitude, and still he waited. "I've waited so long it can't be much longer now," he told me as he said good-bye after almost four hours of nostalgia. “It may be a matter of months.” He shuffled down the middle of the street, wearing the combat boots and faded cap of an old Roman, ignoring the puddles of rain where the light was beginning to decay. Then I had no doubt, if I ever had any at all, that the Saint was Margarito. Without realizing it, by means of his daughter’s incorruptible body and while he was still alive, he had spent twenty-two years fighting for the legitimate cause of his own canonization.

Raymond Carver

FAITH

Cathedral

THIS BLIND MAN, an old friend of my wife's, he was on his way to spend the night. His wife had died. So he was visiting the dead wife's relatives in Connecticut. He called my wife from his in-laws'. Arrangements were made. He would come by train, a five-hour trip, and my wife would meet him at the station. She hadn't seen him since she worked for him one summer in Seattle ten years ago. But she and the blind man had kept in touch. They made tapes and mailed them back and forth. I wasn't enthusiastic about his visit. He was no one I knew. And his being blind bothered me. My idea of blindness came from the movies. In the movies, the blind moved slowly and never laughed. Sometimes they were led by seeing-eye dogs. A blind man in my house was not something I looked forward to.

That summer in Seattle she had needed a job. She didn't have any money. The man she was going to marry at the end of the summer was in officers' training school. He didn't have any money, either. But she was in love with the guy, and he was in love with her, etc. She'd seen something in the paper: HELP WANTED—*Reading to Blind Man*, and a telephone number. She phoned and went over, was hired on the spot. She'd worked with this blind man all summer. She read stuff to him, case studies, reports, that sort of thing. She helped him organize his little office in the county social-service department. They'd become good friends, my wife and the blind man. How do I know these things? She told me. And she told me something else. On her last day in the office, the blind man asked if he could touch her face. She agreed to this. She told me he touched his fingers to every part of her face, her nose—even her neck! She never forgot it. She even tried to write a poem about it. She was always trying to write a poem. She wrote a poem or two every year, usually after something really important had happened to her.

When we first started going out together, she showed me the poem. In the poem, she recalled his fingers and the way they had moved around over her face. In the poem, she talked about what she had felt at the time, about what went through her mind when the blind man touched her nose and lips. I can remember I didn't think much of the poem. Of course, I didn't tell her that. Maybe I just don't understand poetry. I admit it's not the first thing I reach for when I pick up something to read.

Anyway, this man who'd first enjoyed her favors, the officer-to-be, he'd been her childhood sweetheart. So okay. I'm saying that at the end of the summer she let the blind man run his hands over her face, said good-bye to him, married her childhood etc., who was now a commissioned officer, and she moved away from Seattle. But they'd kept in touch, she and the blind man. She made the first contact after a year or so. She called him up one night from an Air Force base in Alabama. She wanted to talk. They talked. He asked her to send him a tape and tell him about her life. She did this. She sent the tape. On the tape, she told the blind man about her husband and about their life together in the military. She told the blind man she loved her husband but she didn't like it where they lived and she didn't like it that he was a part of the military-industrial thing. She told the blind man she'd written a poem and he was in it. She told him that she was writing a poem about what it was like to be an Air Force officer's wife. The poem wasn't finished yet. She was still writing it. The blind man made a tape. He sent her the tape. She made a tape. This went on for years. My wife's officer was posted to one base and then another. She sent tapes from Moody AFB, McGuire, McConnell, and finally Travis, near Sacramento, where one night she got feeling lonely and cut off from people she kept losing in that moving-around life. She got to feeling she couldn't go it another step. She went in and swallowed all the pills and capsules in the medicine chest and washed them down with a bottle of gin. Then she got into a hot bath and passed out.

But instead of dying, she got sick. She threw up. Her officer—why should he have a name? he was the childhood sweetheart, and what more does he want?—came home from somewhere, found her, and called the ambulance. In time, she put it all on a tape and sent the tape to the blind man. Over the years, she put all kinds of stuff on tapes and sent the tapes off lickety-split. Next to writing a poem every year, I think it was her chief means of recreation. On one tape, she told the blind man she'd decided to live away from her officer for a time. On another tape, she told him about her divorce. She and I began going out, and of course she told her blind man about it. She told him everything, or so it seemed to me. Once she asked me if I'd like to hear the latest tape from the blind man. This was a year ago. I was on the tape, she said. So I said okay, I'd listen to it. I got us drinks and we settled down in the living room. We made ready to listen. First she inserted the tape into the player and adjusted a couple of dials. Then she pushed a lever. The tape squeaked and someone began to talk in this loud voice. She lowered the volume. After a few minutes of harmless chitchat, I heard my own name in the mouth of this stranger, this blind man I didn't even know! And then this: "From all you've said about him, I can only conclude—" But we were interrupted, a knock at the door, something, and we didn't ever get back to the tape. Maybe it was just as well. I'd heard all I wanted to.

Now this same blind man was coming to sleep in my house.

"Maybe I could take him bowling," I said to my wife. She was at the draining board doing scalloped potatoes. She put down the knife she was using and turned around.

"If you love me," she said, "you can do this for me. If you don't love me, okay. But if you had a friend, any friend, and the friend came to visit, I'd make him feel comfortable." She wiped her hands with the dish towel.

"I don't have any blind friends," I said.

"You don't have *any* friends," she said. "Period. Besides," she said, "goddamn it, his wife just died! Don't you understand that? The man's lost his wife!"

I didn't answer. She'd told me a little bit about the blind man's wife. Her name was Beulah. Beulah! That's a name for a colored woman.

"Was his wife a Negro?" I asked.

"Are you crazy?" my wife said. "Have you just flipped or something?" She picked up a potato. I saw it hit the floor, then roll under the stove. "What's wrong with you?" she said. "Are you drunk?"

"I'm just asking," I said.

Right then my wife filled me in with more detail than I cared to know. I made a drink and sat at the kitchen table to listen. Pieces of the story began to fall into place.

Beulah had gone to work for the blind man the summer after my wife had stopped working for him. Pretty soon Beulah and the blind man had themselves a church wedding. It was a little wedding—who'd want to go to such a wedding in the first place?—just the two of them, plus the minister and the minister's wife. But it was a church wedding just the same. It was what Beulah had wanted, he'd said. But even then Beulah must have been carrying the cancer in her glands. After they had been inseparable for eight years—my wife's word, *inseparable*—Beulah's health went into a rapid decline. She died in a Seattle hospital room, the blind man sitting beside the bed and holding on to her hand. They'd married, lived and worked together, slept together—had sex, sure—and then the blind man had to bury her. All this without having seen what the goddamned woman looked like. It was beyond my understanding. Hearing this, I felt sorry for the blind man for a little bit. And then I found myself thinking what a pitiful life this woman must have led. Imagine a woman who could never see herself as she was seen in the eyes of her loved one. A woman who could go on day after day and never receive the smallest compliment from her beloved. A woman whose husband could never read the expression on her face, be it misery or something better. Someone who could wear makeup or not—what difference to him? She could, if she wanted, wear green eye shadow around one eye, a straight pin in her nostril, yellow slacks, and purple shoes, no matter. And then to slip off into death, the blind man's hand in her hand, his blind eyes streaming tears—I'm imagining now—her last thought maybe this: that he never even knew what she looked like, and she on an express to the grave. Robert was left with a small insurance policy and half of a twenty-peso Mexican coin. The other half of the coin went into the box with her. Pathetic.

So when the time rolled around, my wife went to the depot to pick him up. With nothing to do but wait—sure, I blamed him for that—I was having a drink and watching the TV when I heard the car pull into the drive. I got up from the sofa with my drink and went to the window to have a look.

I saw my wife laughing as she parked the car. I saw her get out of the car and shut the door. She was still wearing a smile. Just amazing. She went around to the other side of the car to where the blind man was already starting to get out. This blind man, feature this, he was wearing a full beard! A beard on a blind man! Too much, I say. The blind man reached into the backseat and dragged out a suitcase. My wife took his arm, shut the car door, and, talking all the way, moved him down the drive and then up the steps to the front porch. I turned off the TV. I finished my drink, rinsed the glass, dried my hands. Then I went to the door.

My wife said, "I want you to meet Robert. Robert, this is my husband.

I've told you all about him." She was beaming. She had this blind man by his coat sleeve.

The blind man let go of his suitcase and up came his hand.

I took it. He squeezed hard, held my hand, and then he let it go.

"I feel like we've already met," he boomed.

"Likewise," I said. I didn't know what else to say. Then I said, "Welcome. I've heard a lot about you." We began to move then, a little group, from the porch into the living room, my wife guiding him by the arm. The blind man was carrying his suitcase in his other hand. My wife said things like, "To your left here, Robert. That's right. Now watch it, there's a chair. That's it. Sit down right here. This is the sofa. We just bought this sofa two weeks ago."

I started to say something about the old sofa. I'd liked that old sofa. But I didn't say anything. Then I wanted to say something else, small talk, about the scenic ride along the Hudson. How going *to* New York, you should sit on the right-hand side of the train, and coming *from* New York, the left-hand side.

"Did you have a good train ride?" I said. "Which side of the train did you sit on, by the way?"

"What a question, which side!" my wife said. "What's it matter which side?" she said.

"I just asked," I said.

"Right side," the blind man said. "I hadn't been on a train in nearly forty years. Not since I was a kid. With my folks. That's been a long time. I'd nearly forgotten the sensation. I have winter in my beard now," he said. "So I've been told, anyway. Do I look distinguished, my dear?" the blind man said to my wife.

"You look distinguished, Robert," she said. "Robert," she said. "Robert, it's just so good to see you."

My wife finally took her eyes off the blind man and looked at me. I had the feeling she didn't like what she saw. I shrugged.

I've never met, or personally known, anyone who was blind. This blind man was in his late forties, a heavyset, balding man with stooped shoulders, as if he carried a great weight there. He wore brown slacks, brown shoes, a light-brown shirt, a tie, a sports coat. Spiffy. He also had this full beard. But he didn't use a cane and he didn't wear dark glasses. I'd always thought dark glasses were a must for the blind. Fact was, I wished he had a pair. At first glance, his eyes looked like anyone else's eyes. But if you looked close, there was something different about them. Too much white in the iris, for one thing, and the pupils seemed to move around in the sockets without his knowing it or being able to stop it. Creepy. As I stared at his face, I saw the left pupil turn in toward his nose while the other made an effort to keep in one place. But it was only an effort, for that eye was on the roam without his knowing it or wanting it to be.

I said, "Let me get you a drink. What's your pleasure? We have a little of everything. It's one of our pastimes."

"Bub, I'm a Scotch man myself," he said fast enough in this big voice.

"Right," I said. Bub! "Sure you are. I knew it."

He let his fingers touch his suitcase, which was sitting alongside the sofa. He was taking his bearings. I didn't blame him for that.

"I'll move that up to your room," my wife said.

"No, that's fine," the blind man said loudly. "It can go up when I go up."

"A little water with the Scotch?" I said.

"Very little," he said.

"I knew it," I said.

He said, "Just a tad. The Irish actor, Barry Fitzgerald? I'm like that fellow. When I drink water, Fitzgerald said, I drink water. When I drink whiskey, I drink whiskey." My wife laughed. The blind man brought his hand up under his beard. He lifted his beard slowly and let it drop.

I did the drinks, three big glasses of Scotch with a splash of water in each. Then we made ourselves comfortable and talked about Robert's travels. First the long flight from the West Coast to Connecticut, we covered that. Then from Connecticut up here by train. We had another drink considering that leg of the trip.

I remembered having read somewhere that the blind didn't smoke because, as speculation had it, they couldn't see the smoke they exhaled. I thought I knew that much and that much only about blind people. But this blind man smoked his cigarette down to the nubbin and then lit another one. This blind man filled his ashtray and my wife emptied it.

When we sat down at the table for dinner, we had another drink. My wife heaped Robert's plate with cube steak, scalloped potatoes, green beans. I buttered him up two slices of bread. I said, "Here's bread and butter for you." I swallowed some of my drink. "Now let us pray," I said, and the blind man lowered his head. My wife looked at me, her mouth agape. "Pray the phone won't ring and the food doesn't get cold," I said.

We dug in. We ate everything there was to eat on the table. We ate like there was no tomorrow. We didn't talk. We ate. We scarfed. We grazed that table. We were into serious eating. The blind man had right away located his foods, he knew just where everything was on his plate. I watched with admiration as he used his knife and fork on the meat. He'd cut two pieces of meat, fork the meat into his mouth, and then go all out for the scalloped potatoes, the beans next, and then he'd tear off a hunk of buttered bread and eat that. He'd follow this up with a big drink of milk. It didn't seem to bother him to use his fingers once in a while, either.

We finished everything, including half a strawberry pie. For a few moments, we sat as if stunned. Sweat beaded on our faces. Finally, we got up from the table and left the dirty plates. We didn't look back. We took ourselves into the living room and sank into our places again. Robert and my wife sat on the sofa. I took the big chair. We had us two or three more drinks while they talked about the major things that had come to pass for them in the past ten years. For the most part, I just listened. Now and then I joined in. I didn't want him to think I'd left the room, and I didn't want her to think I was feeling left out. They talked of things that had happened to them—to them!—these past ten years. I waited in vain to hear my name on my wife's sweet lips: "And then my dear husband came into my life"—something like that. But I heard nothing of the sort. More talk of Robert. Robert had done a little of everything, it seemed, a regular blind jack-of-all-trades. But most recently he and his wife had had an Amway distributorship, from which, I gathered, they'd earned their living, such as it was. The blind man was also a ham radio operator. He talked in his loud voice about conversations he'd had with fellow operators in Guam, in the Philippines, in Alaska, and even in Tahiti. He said he'd have a lot of friends there if he ever wanted to go visit those places. From time to time, he'd turn his blind face toward me, put his hand under his beard, ask me something. How long had I been in my present position? (Three years.) Did I like my work? (I didn't.) Was I going to stay with it? (What were the options?) Finally, when I thought he was beginning to run down, I got up and turned on the TV.

My wife looked at me with irritation. She was heading toward a boil. Then she looked at the blind man and said, "Robert, do you have a TV?"

The blind man said, "My dear, I have two TVs. I have a color set and a black-and-white thing, an old relic. It's funny, but if I turn the TV on, and I'm always turning it on, I turn on the color set. It's funny, don't you think?"

I didn't know what to say to that. I had absolutely nothing to say to that. No opinion. So I watched the news program and tried to listen to what the announcer was saying.

"This is a color TV," the blind man said. "Don't ask me how, but I can tell."

"We traded up a while ago," I said.

The blind man had another taste of his drink. He lifted his beard, sniffed it, and let it fall. He leaned forward on the sofa. He positioned his ashtray on the coffee table, then put the lighter to his cigarette. He leaned back on the sofa and crossed his legs at the ankles.

My wife covered her mouth, and then she yawned. She stretched. She said, "I think I'll go upstairs and put on my robe. I think I'll change into something else. Robert, you make yourself comfortable," she said.

"I'm comfortable," the blind man said.

"I want you to feel comfortable in this house," she said.

"I am comfortable," the blind man said.

AFTER SHE'D LEFT the room, he and I listened to the weather report and then to the sports roundup. By that time, she'd been gone so long I didn't know if she was going to come back. I thought she might have gone to bed. I wished she'd come back downstairs. I didn't want to be left alone with a blind man. I asked him if he wanted another drink, and he said sure. Then I asked if he wanted to smoke some dope with me. I said I'd just rolled a number. I hadn't, but I planned to do so in about two shakes.

"I'll try some with you," he said.

"Damn right," I said. "That's the stuff."

I got our drinks and sat down on the sofa with him. Then I rolled us two fat numbers. I lit one and passed it. I brought it to his fingers. He took it and inhaled.

"Hold it as long as you can," I said. I could tell he didn't know the first thing.

My wife came back downstairs wearing her pink robe and her pink slippers.

"What do I smell?" she said.

"We thought we'd have us some cannabis," I said.

My wife gave me a savage look. Then she looked at the blind man and said, "Robert, I didn't know you smoked."

He said, "I do now, my dear. There's a first time for everything. But I don't feel anything yet."

"This stuff is pretty mellow," I said. "This stuff is mild. It's dope you can reason with," I said. "It doesn't mess you up."

"Not much it doesn't, bub," he said, and laughed.

My wife sat on the sofa between the blind man and me. I passed her the number. She took it and toked and then passed it back to me. "Which way is this going?" she said. Then she said, "I shouldn't be smoking this. I can hardly keep my eyes open as it is. That dinner did me in. I shouldn't have eaten so much."

"It was the strawberry pie," the blind man said. "That's what did it," he said, and he laughed his big laugh. Then he shook his head.

"There's more strawberry pie," I said.

"Do you want some more, Robert?" my wife said.

"Maybe in a little while," he said.

We gave our attention to the TV. My wife yawned again. She said, "Your bed is made up when you feel like going to bed, Robert. I know you must have had a long day. When you're ready to go to bed, say so." She pulled his arm. "Robert?"

He came to and said, "I've had a real nice time. This beats tapes, doesn't it?"

I said, "Coming at you," and I put the number between his fingers. He inhaled, held the smoke, and then let it go. It was like he'd been doing it since he was nine years old.

"Thanks, bub," he said. "But I think this is all for me. I think I'm beginning to feel it," he said. He held the burning roach out for my wife.

"Same here," she said. "Ditto. Me, too." She took the roach and passed it to me. "I may just sit here for a while between you two guys with my eyes closed. But don't let me bother you, okay? Either one of you. If it bothers you, say so. Otherwise, I may just sit here with my eyes closed until you're ready to go to bed," she said. "Your bed's made up, Robert, when you're ready. It's right next to our room at the top of the stairs. We'll show you up when you're ready. You wake me up now, you guys, if I fall asleep." She said that and then she closed her eyes and went to sleep.

The news progam ended. I got up and changed the channel. I sat back down on the sofa. I wished my wife hadn't pooped out. Her head lay across the back of the sofa, her mouth open. She'd turned so that her robe had slipped from her legs, exposing a juicy thigh. I reached to draw her robe back over her, and it was then that I glanced at the blind man. What the hell! I flipped the robe open again.

"You say when you want some strawberry pie," I said.

"I will," he said.

I said, "Are you tired? Do you want me to take you up to your bed? Are you ready to hit the hay?"

"Not yet," he said. "No, I'll stay up with you, bub. If that's all right. I'll stay up until you're ready to turn in. We haven't had a chance to talk. Know what I mean? I feel like me and her monopolized the evening." He lifted his beard and he let it fall. He picked up his cigarettes and his lighter.

"That's all right," I said. Then I said, "I'm glad for the company."

And I guess I was. Every night I smoked dope and stayed up as long as I could before I fell asleep. My wife and I hardly ever went to bed at the same time. When I did go to sleep, I had these dreams. Sometimes I'd wake up from one of them, my heart going crazy.

Something about the church and the Middle Ages was on the TV. Not your run-of-the-mill TV fare. I wanted to watch something else. I turned to the other channels. But there was nothing on them, either. So I turned back to the first channel and apologized.

"Bub, it's all right," the blind man said. "It's fine with me. Whatever you want to watch is okay. I'm always learning something. Learning never ends. It won't hurt me to learn something tonight. I got ears," he said.

HE DIDN'T SAY anything for a time. He was leaning forward with his head turned at me, his right ear aimed in the direction of the set. Very disconcerting. Now and then his eyelids drooped and then they snapped open again. Now and then he put his fingers into his beard and tugged, like he was thinking about something he was hearing on the television.

On the screen a group of men wearing cowls was being set upon and tormented by men dressed in skeleton costumes and men dressed as devils. The men dressed as devils wore devil masks, horns, and long tails. This pageant was part of a procession. The Englishman who was narrating the thing said it took place in Spain once a year. I tried to explain to the blind man what was happening.

"Skeletons," he said. "I know about skeletons," he said, and he nodded.

The TV showed this one cathedral. Then there was a long, slow look at another one. Finally, the picture switched to the famous one in Paris, with its flying buttresses and its spires reaching up to the clouds. The camera pulled away to show the whole of the cathedral rising above the skyline.

There were times when the Englishman who was telling the thing would shut up, would simply let the camera move around over the cathedrals. Or else the camera would tour the countryside, men in fields walking behind oxen. I waited as long as I could. Then I felt I had to say something. I said, "They're showing the outside of this cathedral now. Gargoyles. Little statues carved to look like monsters. Now I guess they're in Italy. Yeah, they're in Italy. There's paintings on the walls of this one church."

"Are those fresco paintings, bub?" he asked, as he sipped from his drink.

I reached for my glass. But it was empty. I tried to remember what I could remember. "You're asking me are those frescoes?" I said. "That's a good question. I don't know."

The camera moved to a cathedral outside Lisbon. The differences in the Portuguese cathedral compared with the French and Italian were not that great. But they were there. Mostly the interior stuff. Then something occurred to me, and I said, "Something has occurred to me. Do you have any idea what a cathedral is? What they look like, that is? Do you follow me? If somebody says cathedral to you, do you have any notion what they're talking about? Do you know the difference between that and a Baptist church, say?"

He let the smoke dribble from his mouth. "I know they took hundreds of workers fifty or a hundred years to build," he said. "I just heard the man say that, of course. I know generations of the same families worked on a cathedral. I heard him say that, too. The men who began their life's work on them, they never lived to see the completion of their work. In that wise, bub, they're no different from the rest of us, right?" He laughed. Then his eyelids drooped again. His head nodded. He seemed to be snoozing. Maybe he was imagining himself in Portugal. The TV was showing another cathedral now. This one was in Germany. The Englishman's voice droned on. "Cathedrals," the blind man said. He sat up and rolled his head back and forth. "If you want the truth, bub, that's about all I know. What I just said. What I heard him say. But maybe you could describe one to me? I wish you'd do it. I'd like that. If you want to know, I really don't have a good idea."

I stared hard at the shot of the cathedral on the TV. How could I even begin to describe it? But say my life depended on it. Say my life was being threatened by an insane guy who said I had to do it or else.

I stared some more at the cathedral before the picture flipped off into the countryside. There was no use. I turned to the blind man and said, "To begin with, they're very tall." I was looking around the room for clues. "They reach way up. Up and up. Toward the sky. They're so big, some of them, they have to have these supports. To help hold them up, so to speak. These supports are called buttresses. They remind me of viaducts, for some reason. But maybe you don't know viaducts, either? Sometimes the cathedrals have devils and such carved into the front. Sometimes lords and ladies. Don't ask me why this is," I said.

He was nodding. The whole upper part of his body seemed to be moving back and forth.

"I'm not doing so good, am I?" I said.

He stopped nodding and leaned forward on the edge of the sofa. As he listened to me, he was running his fingers through his beard. I wasn't getting through to him, I could see that. But he waited for me to go on just the same. He nodded, like he was trying to encourage me. I tried to think what else to say. "They're really big," I said. "They're massive.

They're built of stone. Marble, too, sometimes. In those olden days, when they built cathedrals, men wanted to be close to God. In those olden days God was an important part of everyone's life. You could tell this from their cathedral-building. I'm sorry," I said, "but it looks like that's the best I can do for you. I'm just no good at it."

"That's all right, bub," the blind man said. "Hey, listen. I hope you don't mind my asking you. Can I ask you something? Let me ask you a simple question, yes or no. I'm just curious and there's no offense. You're my host. But let me ask if you are in any way religious? You don't mind my asking?"

I shook my head. He couldn't see that, though. A wink is the same as a nod to a blind man. "I guess I don't believe in it. In anything. Sometimes it's hard. You know what I'm saying?"

"Sure, I do," he said.

"Right," I said.

The Englishman was still holding forth. My wife sighed in her sleep. She drew a long breath and went on with her sleeping.

"You'll have to forgive me," I said. "But I can't tell you what a cathedral looks like. It just isn't in me to do it. I can't do any more than I've done."

The blind man sat very still, his head down, as he listened to me.

I said, "The truth is, cathedrals don't mean anything special to me. Nothing. Cathedrals. They're something to look at on late-night TV. That's all they are."

It was then that the blind man cleared his throat. He brought something up. He took a handkerchief from his back pocket. Then he said, "I get it, bub. It's okay. It happens. Don't worry about it," he said. "Hey, listen to me. Will you do me a favor? I got an idea. Why don't you find us some heavy paper? And a pen. We'll do something. We'll draw one together. Get us a pen and some heavy paper. Go on, bub, get the stuff," he said.

So I went upstairs. My legs felt like they didn't have any strength in them. They felt like they did after I'd done some running. In my wife's room, I looked around. I found some ballpoints in a little basket on her table. And then I tried to think where to look for the kind of paper he was talking about.

Downstairs, in the kitchen, I found a shopping bag with onion skins in the bottom of the bag. I emptied the bag and shook it. I brought it into the living room and sat down with it near his legs. I moved some things, smoothed the wrinkles from the bag, spread it out on the coffee table.

The blind man got down from the sofa and sat next to me on the carpet.

He ran his fingers over the paper. He went up and down the sides of the paper. The edges, even the edges. He fingered the corners.

"All right," he said. "All right, let's do her."

He found my hand, the hand with the pen. He closed his hand over my hand. "Go ahead, bub, draw," he said. "Draw. You'll see. I'll follow along with you. It'll be okay. Just begin now like I'm telling you. You'll see. Draw," the blind man said.

So I began. First I drew a box that looked like a house. It could have been the house I lived in. Then I put a roof on it. At either end of the roof, I drew spires. Crazy.

"Swell," he said. "Terrific. You're doing fine," he said. "Never thought anything like this could happen in your lifetime, did you, bub? Well, it's a strange life, we all know that. Go on now. Keep it up."

I put in windows with arches. I drew flying buttresses. I hung great doors. I couldn't stop. The TV station went off the air. I put down the pen and closed and opened my fingers. The blind man felt around over the paper. He moved the tips of his fingers over the paper, all over what I had drawn, and he nodded.

"Doing fine," the blind man said.

I took up the pen again, and he found my hand. I kept at it. I'm no artist. But I kept drawing, just the same.

My wife opened up her eyes and gazed at us. She sat up on the sofa, her robe hanging open. She said, "What are you doing? Tell me, I want to know."

I didn't answer her.

The blind man said, "We're drawing a cathedral. Me and him are working on it. Press hard," he said to me. "That's right. That's good," he said. "Sure. You got it, bub. I can tell. You didn't think you could. But you can, can't you? You're cooking with gas now. You know what I'm saying? We're going to really have us something here in a minute. How's the old arm?" he said. "Put some people in there now. What's a cathedral without people?"

My wife said, "What's going on? Robert, what are you doing? What's going on?"

"It's all right," he said to her. "Close your eyes now," the blind man said to me.

I did it. I closed them just like he said.

"Are they closed?" he said. "Don't fudge."

"They're closed," I said.

"Keep them that way," he said. He said, "Don't stop now. Draw."

So we kept on with it. His fingers rode my fingers as my hand went over the paper. It was like nothing else in my life up to now.

Then he said, "I think that's it. I think you got it," he said. "Take a look. What do you think?"

But I had my eyes closed. I thought I'd keep them that way for a little longer. I thought it was something I ought to do.

"Well?" he said. "Are you looking?"

My eyes were still closed. I was in my house. I knew that. But I didn't feel like I was inside anything.

"It's really something," I said.

Flannery O'Connor

FAITH

Parker's Back

PARKER'S WIFE WAS sitting on the front porch floor, snapping beans. Parker was sitting on the step, some distance away, watching her sullenly. She was plain, plain. The skin on her face was thin and drawn as tight as the skin on an onion and her eyes were gray and sharp like the points of two icepicks. Parker understood why he had married her—he couldn't have got her any other way—but he couldn't understand why he stayed with her now. She was pregnant and pregnant women were not his favorite kind. Nevertheless, he stayed as if she had him conjured. He was puzzled and ashamed of himself.

The house they rented sat alone save for a single tall pecan tree on a high embankment overlooking a highway. At intervals a car would shoot past below and his wife's eyes would swerve suspiciously after the sound of it and then come back to rest on the newspaper full of beans in her lap. One of the things she did not approve of was automobiles. In addition to her other bad qualities, she was forever sniffing up sin. She did not smoke or dip, drink whiskey, use bad language or paint her face, and God knew some paint would have improved it, Parker thought. Her being against color, it was the more remarkable she had married him. Sometimes he supposed that she had married him because she meant to save him. At other times he had a suspicion that she actually liked everything she said she didn't. He could account for her one way or another; it was himself he could not understand.

She turned her head in his direction and said, "It's no reason you can't work for a man. It don't have to be a woman."

"Aw shut your mouth for a change," Parker muttered.

If he had been certain she was jealous of the woman he worked for he would have been pleased but more likely she was concerned with the sin that would result if he and the woman took a liking to each other. He had told her that the woman was a hefty young blonde; in fact she was nearly seventy years old and too dried up to have an interest in anything except getting as much work out of him as she could. Not that an old woman didn't sometimes get an interest in a young man, particularly if he was as attractive as Parker felt he was, but this old woman looked at him the same way she looked at her old tractor—as if she had to put up with it because it was all she had. The tractor had broken down the second day Parker was on it and she had set him at once to cutting bushes, saying out of the side of her mouth to the nigger, "Everything he touches, he breaks." She also asked him to wear his shirt when he worked; Parker had removed it even though the day was not sultry; he put it back on reluctantly.

This ugly woman Parker married was his first wife. He had had other women but he had planned never to get himself tied up legally. He had first seen her one morning when his truck broke down on the highway. He had managed to pull it off the road into a neatly swept yard on which sat a peeling two-room house. He got out and opened the hood of the truck and began to study the motor. Parker had an extra sense that told him when there was a woman nearby watching him. After he had leaned over the motor a few minutes, his neck began to prickle. He cast his eye over the empty yard and porch of the house. A woman he could not see was either nearby beyond a clump of honeysuckle or in the house, watching him out the window.

Suddenly Parker began to jump up and down and fling his hand about as if he had mashed it in the machinery. He doubled over and held his hand close to his chest. "God dammit!" he hollered, "Jesus Christ in hell! Jesus God Almighty damm! God dammit to hell!" he went on, flinging out the same few oaths over and over as loud as he could.

Without warning a terrible bristly claw slammed the side of his face and he fell backwards on the hood of the truck. "You don't talk no filth here!" a voice close to him shrilled.

Parker's vision was so blurred that for an instant he thought he had been attacked by some creature from above, a giant hawk-eyed angel wielding a hoary weapon. As his sight cleared, he saw before him a tall raw-boned girl with a broom.

"I hurt my hand," he said. "I *hurt* my hand." He was so incensed that he forgot that he hadn't hurt his hand. "My hand may be broke," he growled although his voice was still unsteady.

"Lemme see it," the girl demanded.

Parker stuck out his hand and she came closer and looked at it. There was no mark on the palm and she took the hand and turned it over. Her own hand was dry and hot and rough and Parker felt himself jolted back to life by her touch. He looked more closely at her. I don't want nothing to do with this one, he thought.

The girl's sharp eyes peered at the back of the stubby reddish hand she held. There emblazoned in red and blue was a tattooed eagle perched on a cannon. Parker's sleeve was rolled to the elbow. Above the eagle a serpent was coiled about a shield and in the spaces between the eagle and the serpent there were hearts, some with arrows through them. Above the serpent there was a spread hand of cards. Every space on the skin of

Parker's arm, from wrist to elbow, was covered in some loud design. The girl gazed at this with an almost stupefied smile of shock, as if she had accidentally grasped a poisonous snake; she dropped the hand.

"I got most of my other ones in foreign parts," Parker said. "These here I mostly got in the United States. I got my first one when I was only fifteen year old."

"Don't tell me," the girl said, "I don't like it. I ain't got any use for it."

"You ought to see the ones you can't see," Parker said and winked.

Two circles of red appeared like apples on the girl's cheeks and softened her appearance. Parker was intrigued. He did not for a minute think that she didn't like the tattoos. He had never yet met a woman who was not attracted to them.

Parker was fourteen when he saw a man in a fair, tattooed from head to foot. Except for his loins which were girded with a panther hide, the man's skin was patterned in what seemed from Parker's distance—he was near the back of the tent, standing on a bench—a single intricate design of brilliant color. The man, who was small and sturdy, moved about on the platform, flexing his muscles so that the arabesque of men and beasts and flowers on his skin appeared to have a subtle motion of its own. Parker was filled with emotion, lifted up as some people are when the flag passes. He was a boy whose mouth habitually hung open. He was heavy and earnest, as ordinary as a loaf of bread. When the show was over, he had remained standing on the bench, staring where the tattooed man had been, until the tent was almost empty.

Parker had never before felt the least motion of wonder in himself. Until he saw the man at the fair, it did not enter his head that there was anything out of the ordinary about the fact that he existed. Even then it did not enter his head, but a peculiar unease settled in him. It was as if a blind boy had been turned so gently in a different direction that he did not know his destination had been changed.

He had his first tattoo sometime after—the eagle perched on the cannon. It was done by a local artist. It hurt very little, just enough to make it appear to Parker to be worth doing. This was peculiar too for before he had thought that only what did not hurt was worth doing. The next year he quit school because he was sixteen and could. He went to the trade school for a while, then he quit the trade school and worked for six months in a garage. The only reason he worked at all was to pay for more tattoos. His mother worked in a laundry and could support him, but she would not pay for any tattoo except her name on a heart, which he had put on, grumbling. However, her name was Betty Jean and nobody had to know it was his mother. He found out that the tattoos were attractive to the kind of girls he liked but who had never liked him before. He began to drink beer and get in fights. His mother wept over what was becoming of him. One night she dragged him off to a revival with her, not telling him where they were going. When he saw the big lighted church, he jerked out of her grasp and ran. The next day he lied about his age and joined the navy.

Parker was large for the tight sailor's pants but the silly white cap, sitting low on his forehead, made his face by contrast look thoughtful and almost intense. After a month or two in the navy, his mouth ceased to hang open. His features hardened into the features of a man. He stayed in the navy five years and seemed a natural part of the gray mechanical ship, except for his eyes, which were the same pale slate color as the ocean and reflected the immense spaces around him as if they were a microcosm of the mysterious sea. In port Parker wandered about comparing the run-down places he was in to Birmingham, Alabama. Everywhere he went he picked up more tattoos.

He had stopped having lifeless ones like anchors and crossed rifles. He had a tiger and a panther on each shoulder, a cobra coiled about a torch on his chest, hawks on his thighs, Elizabeth II and Philip over where his stomach and liver were respectively. He did not care much what the subject was so long as it was colorful; on his abdomen he had a few obscenities but only because that seemed the proper place for them. Parker would be satisfied with each tattoo about a month, then something about it that had attracted him would wear off. Whenever a decent-sized mirror was available, he would get in front of it and study his overall look. The effect was not of one intricate arabesque of colors but of something haphazard and botched. A huge dissatisfaction would come over him and he would go off and find another tattooist and have another space filled up. The front of Parker was almost completely covered but there were no tattoos on his back. He had no desire for one anywhere he could not readily see it himself. As the space on the front of him for tattoos decreased, his dissatisfaction grew and became general.

After one of his furloughs, he didn't go back to the navy but remained away without official leave, drunk, in a rooming house in a city he did not know. His dissatisfaction, from being chronic and latent, had suddenly become acute and raged in him. It was as if the panther and the lion and the serpents and the eagles and the hawks had penetrated his skin and lived inside him in a raging warfare. The navy caught up with him, put him in the brig for nine months and then gave him a dishonorable discharge.

After that Parker decided that country air was the only kind fit to breathe. He rented the shack on the embankment and bought the old truck and took various jobs which he kept as long as it suited him. At the time he met his future wife, he was buying apples by the bushel and selling them for the same price by the pound to isolated homesteaders on back country roads.

"All that there," the woman said, pointing to his arm, "is no better than what a fool Indian would do. It's a heap of vanity." She seemed to have found the word she wanted. "Vanity of vanities," she said.

Well what the hell do I care what she thinks of it? Parker asked himself, but he was plainly bewildered. "I reckon you like one of these better than another anyway," he said, dallying until he thought of something that would impress her. He thrust the arm back at her. "Which you like best?"

"None of them," she said, "but the chicken is not as bad as the rest."

"What chicken?" Parker almost yelled.

She pointed to the eagle.

"That's an eagle," Parker said. "What fool would waste their time having a chicken put on themself?"

"What fool would have any of it?" the girl said and turned away. She went slowly back to the house and left him there to get going. Parker remained for almost five minutes, looking agape at the dark door she had entered.

The next day he returned with a bushel of apples. He was not one to be outdone by anything that looked like her. He liked women with meat on them, so you didn't feel their muscles, much less their old bones. When he arrived, she was sitting on the top step and the yard was full of children, all as thin and poor as herself; Parker remembered it was Saturday. He hated to be making up to a woman when there were children around, but it was fortunate he had brought the bushel of apples off the truck. As the children approached him to see what he carried, he gave each child an apple and told it to get lost; in that way he cleared out the whole crowd.

The girl did nothing to acknowledge his presence. He might have been a stray pig or goat that had wandered into the yard and she too tired to take up the broom and send it off. He set the bushel of apples down next to her on the step. He sat down on a lower step.

"Hep yourself," he said, nodding at the basket; then he lapsed into silence.

She took an apple quickly as if the basket might disappear if she didn't make haste. Hungry people made Parker nervous. He had always had plenty to eat himself. He grew very uncomfortable. He reasoned he had nothing to say so why should he say it? He could not think now why he had come or why he didn't go before he wasted another bushel of apples on the crowd of children. He supposed they were her brothers and sisters.

She chewed the apple slowly but with a kind of relish of concentration, bent slightly but looking out ahead. The view from the porch stretched off across a long incline studded with ironweed and across the highway to a vast vista of hills and one small mountain. Long views depressed Parker. You look out into space like that and you begin to feel as if someone were after you, the navy or the government or religion.

"Who them children belong to, you?" he said at length.

"I ain't married yet," she said. "They belong to momma." She said it as if it were only a matter of time before she would be married.

Who in God's name would marry her? Parker thought.

A large barefooted woman with a wide gap-toothed face appeared in the door behind Parker. She had apparently been there for several minutes.

"Good evening," Parker said.

The woman crossed the porch and picked up what was left of the bushel of apples. "We thank you," she said and returned with it into the house.

"That your old woman?" Parker muttered.

The girl nodded. Parker knew a lot of sharp things he could have said like "You got my sympathy," but he was gloomily silent. He just sat there, looking at the view. He thought he must be coming down with something.

"If I pick up some peaches tomorrow I'll bring you some," he said.

"I'll be much obliged to you," the girl said.

Parker had no intention of taking any basket of peaches back there but the next day he found himself doing it. He and the girl had almost nothing to say to each other. One thing he did say was, "I ain't got any tattoo on my back."

"What you got on it?" the girl said.

"My shirt," Parker said. "Haw."

"Haw, haw," the girl said politely.

Parker thought he was losing his mind. He could not believe for a minute that he was attracted to a woman like this. She showed not the least interest in anything but what he brought until he appeared the third time with two cantaloups. "What's your name?" she asked.

"O. E. Parker," he said.

"What does the O.E. stand for?"

"You can just call me O.E.," Parker said. "Or Parker. Don't nobody call me by my name."

"What's it stand for?" she persisted.

"Never mind," Parker said. "What's yours?"

"I'll tell you when you tell me what them letters are the short of," she said. There was just a hint of flirtatiousness in her tone and it went rapidly to Parker's head. He had never revealed the name to any man or woman, only to the files of the navy and the government, and it was on his baptismal record which he got at the age of a month; his mother was a Methodist. When the name leaked out of the navy files, Parker narrowly missed killing the man who used it.

"You'll go blab it around," he said.

"I'll swear I'll never tell nobody," she said. "On God's holy word I swear it."

Parker sat for a few minutes in silence. Then he reached for the girl's neck, drew her ear close to his mouth and revealed the name in low voice.

"Obadiah," she whispered. Her face slowly brightened as if the name came as a sign to her. "Obadiah," she said.

The name still stank in Parker's estimation.

"Obadiah Elihue," she said in a reverent voice.

"If you call me that aloud, I'll bust your head open," Parker said. "What's yours?"

"Sarah Ruth Cates," she said.

"Glad to meet you, Sarah Ruth," Parker said.

Sarah Ruth's father was a Straight Gospel preacher but he was away, spreading it in Florida. Her mother did not seem to mind his attention to the girl so long as he brought a basket of something with him when he came. As for Sarah Ruth herself, it was plain to Parker after he had visited three times that she was crazy about him. She liked him even though she insisted that pictures on the skin were vanity of vanities and even after hearing him curse, and even after she had asked him if he was saved and he had replied that he didn't see it was anything in particular to save him from. After that, inspired, Parker had said, "I'd be saved enough if you was to kiss me."

She scowled. "That ain't being saved," she said.

Not long after that she agreed to take a ride in his truck. Parker parked it on a deserted road and suggested to her that they lie down together in the back of it.

"Not until after we're married," she said—just like that.

"Oh that ain't necessary," Parker said and as he reached for her, she thrust him away with such force that the door of the truck came off and he found himself flat on his back on the ground. He made up his mind then and there to have nothing further to do with her.

They were married in the County Ordinary's office because Sarah Ruth thought churches were idolatrous. Parker had no opinion about that one way or the other. The Ordinary's office was lined with card-board file boxes and record books with dusty yellow slips of paper hanging on out of them. The Ordinary was an old woman with red hair who had held office for forty years and looked as dusty as her books. She married them from behind the iron grill of a stand-up desk and when she finished, she said with a flourish, "Three dollars and fifty cents and till death do you part!" and yanked some forms out of a machine.

Marriage did not change Sarah Ruth a jot and it made Parker gloomier than ever. Every morning he decided he had had enough and would not return that night; every night he returned. Whenever Parker couldn't stand the way he felt, he would have another tattoo, but the only surface left on him now was his back. To see a tattoo on his own back he would have to get two mirrors and stand between them in just the correct position and this seemed to Parker a good way to make an idiot of himself. Sarah Ruth who, if she had had better sense, could have enjoyed a tattoo on his back, would not even look at the ones he had elsewhere. When he attempted to point out especial details of them, she would shut her eyes tight and turn her back as well. Except in total darkness, she preferred Parker dressed and with his sleeves rolled down.

"At the judgement seat of God, Jesus is going to say to you, 'What you been doing all your life besides have pictures drawn all over you?'" she said.

"You don't fool me none," Parker said, "you're just afraid that hefty girl I work for'll like me so much she'll say, 'Come on, Mr. Parker, let's you and me . . .'"

"You're tempting sin," she said, "and at the judgement seat of God you'll have to answer for that too. You ought to go back to selling the fruits of the earth."

Parker did nothing much when he was at home but listen to what the judgement seat of God would be like for him if he didn't change his ways. When he could, he broke in with tales of the hefty girl he worked for. "'Mr. Parker,'" he said she said, "'I hired you for your brains.'" (She had added, "So why don't you use them?")

"And you should have seen her face the first time she saw me without my shirt," he said. "'Mr. Parker,' she said, 'you're a walking panner-rammer!'" This had, in fact, been her remark but it had been delivered out of one side of her mouth.

Dissatisfaction began to grow so great in Parker that there was no containing it outside of a tattoo. It had to be his back. There was no help for it. A dim half-formed inspiration began to work in his mind. He visualized having a tattoo put there that Sarah Ruth would not be able to resist—a religious subject. He thought of an open book with HOLY BIBLE tattooed under it and an actual verse printed on the page. This seemed just the thing for a while; then he began to hear her say, "Ain't I already got a real Bible? What you think I want to read the same verse over and over for when I can read it all?" He needed something better even than the Bible! He thought about it so much that he began to lose sleep. He was already losing flesh—Sarah Ruth just threw food in the pot and let it boil. Not knowing for certain why he continued to stay with a woman who was both ugly and pregnant and no cook made him generally nervous and irritable, and he developed a little tic in the side of his face.

Once or twice he found himself turning around abruptly as if someone were trailing him. He had had a granddaddy who had ended in the state mental hospital, although not until he was seventy-five, but as urgent as it might be for him to get a tattoo, it was just as urgent that he get exactly the right one to bring Sarah Ruth to heel. As he continued to worry over it, his eyes took on a hollow preoccupied expression. The old woman he worked for told him that if he couldn't keep his mind on what he was doing, she knew where she could find a fourteen-year-old colored boy who could. Parker was too preoccupied even to be offended. At any time previous, he would have left her then and there, saying dryly, "Well, you go ahead on and get him then."

Two or three mornings later he was baling hay with the old woman's sorry baler and her broken-down tractor in a large field, cleared save for one enormous old tree standing in the middle of it. The old woman was the kind who would not cut down a large old tree because it was a large old tree. She had pointed it out to Parker as if he didn't have eyes and told him to be careful not to hit it as the machine picked up hay near it. Parker began at the outside of the field and made circles inward toward it. He had to get off the tractor every now and then and untangle the baling cord or kick a rock out of the way. The old woman had told him to carry the rocks to the edge of the field, which he did when she was there watching. When he thought he could make it, he ran over them. As he circled the field his mind was on a suitable design for his back. The sun, the size of a golf ball, began to switch regularly from in front to behind him, but he appeared to see it both places as if he had eyes in the back of his head. All at once he saw the tree reaching out to grasp him. A ferocious thud propelled him into the air, and he heard himself yelling in an unbelievably loud voice, "*God Above!*"

He landed on his back while the tractor crashed upside down into the tree and burst into flame. The first thing Parker saw were his shoes, quickly being eaten by the fire; one was caught under the tractor, the other was some distance away, burning by itself. He was not in them. He could feel the hot breath of the burning tree on his face. He scrambled backwards, still sitting, his eyes cavernous, and if he had known how to cross himself he would have done it.

His truck was on a dirt road at the edge of the field. He moved toward it, still sitting, still backwards, but faster and faster; halfway to it he got up and began a kind of forward-bent run from which he collapsed on his knees twice. His legs felt like two old rusted rain gutters. He reached the truck finally and took off in it, zigzagging up the road. He drove past his house on the embankment and straight for the city, fifty miles distant.

Parker did not allow himself to think on the way to the city. He only knew that there had been a great change in his life, a leap forward into a worse unknown, and that there was nothing he could do about it. It was for all intents accomplished.

The artist had two large cluttered rooms over a chiropodist's office on a back street. Parker, still barefooted, burst silently in on him at a little after three in the afternoon. The artist, who was about Parker's own age—twenty-eight—but thin and bald, was behind a small drawing table, tracing a design in green ink. He looked up with an annoyed glance and did not seem to recognize Parker in the hollow-eyed creature before him.

"Let me see the book you got with all the pictures of God in it," Parker said breathlessly. "The religious one."

The artist continued to look at him with his intellectual, superior stare. "I don't put tattoos on drunks," he said.

"You know me!" Parker cried indignantly. "I'm O. E. Parker! You done work for me before and I always paid!"

The artist looked at him another moment as if he were not altogether sure. "You've fallen off some," he said. "You must have been in jail."

"Married," Parker said.

"Oh," said the artist. With the aid of mirrors the artist had tattooed on the top of his head a miniature owl, perfect in every detail. It was about the size of a half-dollar and served him as a showpiece. There were cheaper artists in town but Parker had never wanted anything but the best. The artist went over to a cabinet at the back of the room and began to look over some art books. "Who are you interested in?" he said, "saints, angels, Christs or what?"

"God," Parker said.

"Father, Son or Spirit?"

"Just God," Parker said impatiently. "Christ. I don't care. Just so it's God."

The artist returned with a book. He moved some papers off another table and put the book down on it and told Parker to sit down and see what he liked. "The up-t-date ones are in the back," he said.

Parker sat down with the book and wet his thumb. He began to go through it, beginning at the back where the up-to-date pictures were. Some of them he recognized—The Good Shepherd, Forbid Them Not, The Smiling Jesus, Jesus the Physician's Friend, but he kept turning rapidly backwards and the pictures became less and less reassuring. One showed a gaunt green dead face streaked with blood. One was yellow with sagging purple eyes. Parker's heart began to beat faster and faster until it appeared to be roaring inside him like a great generator. He flipped the pages quickly, feeling that when he reached the one ordained, a sign would come. He continued to flip through until he had almost reached the front of the book. On one of the pages a pair of eyes glanced at him swiftly. Parker sped on, then stopped. His heart too appeared to cut off; there was absolute silence. It said as plainly as if silence were a language itself, GO BACK.

Parker returned to the picture—the haloed head of a flat stern Byzantine Christ with all-demanding eyes. He sat there trembling; his heart began slowly to beat again as if it were being brought to life by a subtle power.

"You found what you want?" the artist asked.

Parker's throat was too dry to speak. He got up and thrust the book at the artist, opened at the picture.

"That'll cost you plenty," the artist said. "You don't want all those little blocks though, just the outline and some better features."

"Just like it is," Parker said, "just like it is or nothing."

"It's your funeral," the artist said, "but I don't do that kind of work for nothing."

"How much?" Parker asked.

"It'll take maybe two days' work."

"How much?" Parker said.

"On time or cash?" the artist asked. Parker's other jobs had been on time, but he had paid.

"Ten down and ten for every day it takes," the artist said.

Parker drew ten dollar bills out of his wallet; he had three left in.

"You come back in the morning," the artist said, putting the money in his own pocket. "First I'll have to trace that out of the book."

"No no!" Parker said. "Trace it now or gimme my money back," and his eyes blared as if he were ready for a fight.

The artist agreed. Anyone stupid enough to want a Christ on his back, he reasoned, would be just as likely as not to change his mind the next minute, but once the work was begun he could hardly do so.

While he worked on the tracing, he told Parker to go wash his back at the sink with the special soap he used there. Parker did it and returned to pace back and forth across the room, nervously flexing his shoulders. He wanted to go look at the picture again but at the same time he did not want to. The artist got up finally and had Parker lie down on the table. He swabbed his back with ethyl chloride and then began to outline the head on it with his iodine pencil. Another hour passed before he took up his electric instrument. Parker felt no particular pain. In Japan he had had a tattoo of the Buddha done on his upper arm with ivory needles; in Burma, a little brown root of a man had made a peacock on each of his knees using thin pointed sticks, two feet long; amateurs had worked on him with pins and soot. Parker was usually so relaxed and easy under the hand of the artist that he often went to sleep, but this time he remained awake, every muscle taut.

At midnight the artist said he was ready to quit. He propped one mirror, four feet square, on a table by the wall and took a smaller mirror off the lavatory wall and put it in Parker's hands. Parker stood with his back to the one on the table and moved the other until he saw a flashing burst of color reflected from his back. It was almost completely covered with little red and blue and ivory and saffron squares; from them he made out the lineaments of the face—a mouth, the beginning of heavy brows, a straight nose, but the face was empty; the eyes had not yet been put in. The impression for the moment was almost as if the artist had tricked him and done the Physician's Friend.

"It don't have eyes," Parker cried out.

"That'll come," the artist said, "in due time. We have another day to go on it yet."

Parker spent the night on a cot at the Haven of Light Christian Mission. He found these the best places to stay in the city because they were free and included a meal of sorts. He got the last available cot and because he was still barefooted, he accepted a pair of secondhand shoes which, in his confusion, he put on to go to bed; he was still shocked from all that had happened to him. All night he lay awake in the long dormitory of cots with lumpy figures on them. The only light was from a phosphorescent cross glowing at the end of the room. The tree reached out to grasp him again, then burst into flame; the shoe burned quietly by itself; the eyes in the book said to him distinctly GO BACK and at the same time did not utter a sound. He wished that he were not in this city, not in this Haven of Light Mission, not in a bed by himself. He longed miserably for Sarah Ruth. Her sharp tongue and icepick eyes were the only comfort he could bring to mind. He decided he was losing it. Her eyes appeared soft and dilatory compared with the eyes in the book, for even though he could not summon up the exact look of those eyes, he could still feel their penetration. He felt as though, under their gaze, he was as transparent as the wing of a fly.

The tattooist had told him not to come until ten in the morning, but when he arrived at that hour, Parker was sitting in the dark hallway on the floor, waiting for him. He had decided upon getting up that, once the tattoo was on him, he would not look at it, that all his sensations of the day and night before were those of a crazy man and that he would return to doing things according to his own sound judgement.

The artist began where he left off. "One thing I want to know," he said presently as he worked over Parker's back, "why do you want this on you? Have you gone and got religion? Are you saved?" he asked in a mocking voice.

Parker's throat felt salty and dry. "Naw," he said, "I ain't got no use for none of that. A man can't save his self from whatever it is he don't deserve none of my sympathy." These words seemed to leave his mouth like wraiths and to evaporate at once as if he had never uttered them.

"Then why . . ."

"I married this woman that's saved," Parker said. "I never should have done it. I ought to leave her. She's done gone and got pregnant."

"That's too bad," the artist said. "Then it's her making you have this tattoo."

"Naw," Parker said, "she don't know nothing about it. It's a surprise for her."

"You think she'll like it and lay off you a while?"

"She can't hep herself," Parker said. "She can't say she don't like the looks of God." He decided he had told the artist enough of his business. Artists were all right in their place but he didn't like them poking their noses into the affairs of regular people. "I didn't get no sleep last night," he said. "I think I'll get some now."

That closed the mouth of the artist but it did not bring him any sleep. He lay there, imagining how Sarah Ruth would be struck speechless by the face on his back and every now and then this would be interrupted by a vision of the tree of fire and his empty shoe burning beneath it.

The artist worked steadily until nearly four o'clock, not stopping to have lunch, hardly pausing with the electric instrument except to wipe the dripping dye off Parker's back as he went along. Finally he finished. "You can get up and look at it now," he said.

Parker sat up but he remained on the edge of the table.

The artist was pleased with his work and wanted Parker to look at it at once. Instead Parker continued to sit on the edge of the table, bent forward slightly but with a vacant look. "What ails you?" the artist said. "Go look at it."

"Ain't nothing ail me," Parker said in a sudden belligerent voice. "That tattoo ain't going nowhere. It'll be there when I get there." He reached for his shirt and began gingerly to put it on.

The artist took him roughly by the arm and propelled him between the two mirrors. "Now *look*," he said, angry at having his work ignored.

Parker looked, turned white and moved away. The eyes in the reflected face continued to look at him—still, straight, all-demanding, enclosed in silence.

"It was your idea, remember," the artist said. "I would have advised something else."

Parker said nothing. He put on his shirt and went out the door while the artist shouted, "I'll expect all of my money!"

Parker headed toward a package shop on the corner. He bought a pint of whiskey and took it into a nearby alley and drank it all in five minutes. Then he moved on to a pool hall nearby which he frequented when he came to the city. It was a well-lighted barnlike place with a bar up one side and gambling machines on the other and pool tables in the back. As soon as Parker entered, a large man in a red-and-black-checkered shirt hailed him by slapping him on the back and yelling, "Yeyyyyyy boy! O. E. Parker!"

Parker was not yet ready to be struck on the back. "Lay off," he said, "I got a fresh tattoo there."

"What you got this time?" the man asked and then yelled to a few at the machines. "O.E.'s got him another tattoo."

"Nothing special this time," Parker said and slunk over to a machine that was not being used.

"Come on," the big man said, "let's have a look at O.E.'s tattoo," and while Parker squirmed in their hands, they pulled up his shirt. Parker felt all the hands drop away instantly and his shirt fell again like a veil over the face. There was a silence in the pool room which seemed to Parker to grow from the circle around him until it extended to the foundations under the building and upward through the beams in the roof.

Finally someone said, "Christ!" Then they all broke into noise at once. Parker turned around, an uncertain grin on his face.

"Leave it to O.E.!" the man in the checkered shirt said. "That boy's a real card!"

"Maybe he's gone and got religion," someone yelled.

"Not on your life," Parker said.

"O.E.'s got religion and is witnessing for Jesus, ain't you, O.E.?" a little man with a piece of cigar in his mouth said wryly. "An o-riginal way to do it if I ever saw one."

"Leave it to Parker to think of a new one!" the fat man said.

"Yyeeeeeeyyyyyyy boy!" someone yelled and they all began to whistle and curse in compliment until Parker said, "Aaa shut up."

"What'd you do it for?" somebody asked.

"For laughs," Parker said. "What's it to you?"

"Why ain't you laughing then?" somebody yelled. Parker lunged into the midst of them and like a whirlwind on a summer's day there began a fight that raged amid overturned tables and swinging fists until two of them grabbed him and ran to the door with him and threw him out. Then a calm descended on the pool hall as nerve-shattering as if the long barnlike room were the ship from which Jonah had been cast into the sea.

Parker sat for a long time on the ground in the alley behind the pool hall, examining his soul. He saw it as a spider web of facts and lies that was not at all important to him but which appeared to be necessary in spite of his opinion. The eyes that were now forever on his back were eyes to be obeyed. He was as certain of it as he had ever been of anything. Throughout his life, grumbling and sometimes cursing, often afraid, once in rapture, Parker had obeyed whatever instinct of this kind had come to him—in rapture when his spirit had lifted at the sight of the tattooed man at the fair, afraid when he had joined the navy, grumbling when he had married Sarah Ruth.

The thought of her brought him slowly to his feet. She would know what he had to do. She would clear up the rest of it, and she would at least be pleased. It seemed to him that, all along, that was what he wanted, to please her. His truck was still parked in front of the building where the artist had his place, but it was not far away. He got in it and drove out of the city and into the country night. His head was almost clear of liquor and he observed that his dissatisfaction was gone, but he felt not quite like himself. It was as if he were himself but a stranger to himself, driving into a new country though everything he saw was familiar to him, even at night.

He arrived finally at the house on the embankment, pulled the truck under the pecan tree and got out. He made as much noise as possible to assert that he was still in charge here, that his leaving her for a night without word meant nothing except it was the way he did things. He slammed the car door, stamped up the two steps and across the porch and rattled the doorknob. It did not respond to his touch. "Sarah Ruth!" he yelled, "let me in."

There was no lock on the door and she had evidently placed the back of a chair against the knob. He began to beat on the door and rattle the knob at the same time.

He heard the bed springs screak and bent down and put his head to the keyhole, but it was stopped up with paper. "Let me in!" he hollered, bamming on the door again. "What you got me locked out for?"

A sharp voice close to the door said, "Who's there?"

"Me," Parker said, "O.E."

He waited a moment.

"Me," he said impatiently, "O.E."

Still no sound from inside.

He tried once more. "O.E.," he said, bamming the door two or three more times. "O. E. Parker. You know me."

There was a silence. Then the voice said slowly, "I don't know no O.E."

"Quit fooling," Parker pleaded. "You ain't got any business doing me this way. It's me, old O.E., I'm back. You ain't afraid of me."

"Who's there?" the same unfeeling voice said.

Parker turned his head as if he expected someone behind him to give him the answer. The sky had lightened slightly and there were two or three streaks of yellow floating above the horizon. Then as he stood there, a tree of light burst over the skyline.

Parker fell back against the door as if he had been pinned there by a lance.

"Who's there?" the voice from inside said and there was a quality about it now that seemed final. The knob rattled and the voice said peremptorily, "Who's there, I ast you?"

Parker bent down and put his mouth near the stuffed keyhole. "Obadiah," he whispered and all at once he felt the light pouring through him, turning his spider-web soul into a perfect arabesque of colors, a garden of trees and birds and beasts.

"Obadiah Elihue!" he whispered.

The door opened and he stumbled in. Sarah Ruth loomed there, hands on her hips. She began at once, "That was no hefty blonde woman you was working for and you'll have to pay her every penny on her tractor you busted up. She don't keep insurance on it. She came here and her and me had us a long talk and I . . ."

Trembling, Parker set about lighting the kerosene lamp.

"What's the matter with you, wasting that kerosene this near daylight?" she demanded. "I ain't got to look at you."

A yellow glow enveloped them. Parker put the match down and began to unbutton his shirt.

"And you ain't going to have none of me this near morning," she said.

"Shut your mouth," he said quietly. "Look at this and then I don't want to hear no more out of you." He removed the shirt and turned his back to her.

"Another picture," Sarah Ruth growled. "I might have known you was off after putting some more trash on yourself."

Parker's knees went hollow under him. He wheeled around and cried, "Look at it! Don't just say that! *Look* at it!"

"I done looked," she said.

"Don't you know who it is?" he cried in anguish.

"No, who is it?" Sarah Ruth said. "It ain't anybody I know."

"It's him," Parker said.

"Him who?"

"God!" Parker cried.

"God? God don't look like that!"

"What do you know how he looks?" Parker moaned. "You ain't seen him."

"He don't *look*," Sarah Ruth said. "He's a spirit. No man shall see his face."

"Aw listen," Parker groaned, "this is just a picture of him."

"Idolatry!" Sarah Ruth screamed. "Idolatry! Enflaming yourself with idols under every green tree! I can put up with lies and vanity but I don't want no idolator in this house!" and she grabbed up the broom and began to thrash him across the shoulders with it.

Parker was too stunned to resist. He sat there and let her beat him until she had nearly knocked him senseless and large welts had formed on the face of the tattooed Christ. Then he staggered up and made for the door.

She stamped the broom two or three times on the floor and went to the window and shook it out to get the taint of him off it. Still gripping it, she looked toward the pecan tree and her eyes hardened still more. There he was—who called himself Obadiah Elihue—leaning against the tree, crying like a baby.

Bernard Malamud

FAITH

Angel Levine

MANISCHEVITZ, A TAILOR, in his fifty-first year suffered many reverses and indignities. Previously a man of comfortable means, he overnight lost all he had, when his establishment caught fire, after a metal container of cleaning fluid exploded, and burned to the ground. Although Manischevitz was insured against fire, damage suits by two customers who had been hurt in the flames deprived him of every penny he had saved. At almost the same time, his son, of much promise, was killed in the war, and his daughter, without so much as a word of warning, married a lout and disappeared with him as off the face of the earth. Thereafter Manischevitz was victimized by excruciating backaches and found himself unable to work even as a presser—the only kind of work available to him—for more than an hour or two daily, because beyond that the pain from standing was maddening. His Fanny, a good wife and mother, who had taken in washing and sewing, began before his eyes to waste away. Suffering shortness of breath, she at last became seriously ill and took to her bed. The doctor, a former customer of Manischevitz, who out of pity treated them, at first had difficulty diagnosing her ailment, but later put it down as hardening of the arteries at an advanced stage. He took Manischevitz aside, prescribed complete rest for her, and in whispers gave him to know there was little hope.

Throughout his trials Manischevitz had remained somewhat stoic, almost unbelieving that all this had descended on his head, as if it were happening, let us say, to an acquaintance or some distant relative; it was in sheer quantity of woe, incomprehensible. It was also ridiculous, unjust, and because he had always been a religious man, an affront to God. Manischevitz believed this in all his suffering. When his burden had grown too crushingly heavy to be borne he prayed in his chair with shut hollow eyes: "My dear God, sweetheart, did I deserve that this should happen to me?" Then recognizing the worthlessness of it, he set aside the complaint and prayed humbly for assistance: "Give Fanny back her health, and to me for myself that I shouldn't feel pain in every step. Help now or tomorrow is too late." And Manischevitz wept.

MANISCHEVITZ'S FLAT, WHICH he had moved into after the disastrous fire, was a meager one, furnished with a few sticks of chairs, a table, and bed, in one of the poorer sections of the city. There were three rooms: a small, poorly papered living room; an apology for a kitchen with a wooden icebox; and the comparatively large bedroom where Fanny lay in a sagging secondhand bed, gasping for breath. The bedroom was the warmest room in the house and it was here, after his outburst to God, that Manischevitz, by the light of two small bulbs overhead, sat reading his Jewish newspaper. He was not truly reading because his thoughts were everywhere; however the print offered a convenient resting place for his eyes, and a word or two, when he permitted himself to comprehend them, had the momentary effect of helping him forget his troubles. After a short while he discovered, to his surprise, that he was actively scanning the news, searching for an item of great interest to him.

Exactly what he thought he would read he couldn't say—until he realized, with some astonishment, that he was expecting to discover something about himself. Manischevitz put his paper down and looked up with the distinct impression that someone had come into the apartment, though he could not remember having heard the sound of the door opening. He looked around: the room was very still, Fanny sleeping, for once, quietly. Half frightened, he watched her until he was satisfied she wasn't dead; then, still disturbed by the thought of an unannounced visitor, he stumbled into the living room and there had the shock of his life, for at the table sat a black man reading a newspaper he had folded up to fit into one hand.

"What do you want here?" Manischevitz asked in fright.

The Negro put down the paper and glanced up with a gentle expression. "Good evening." He seemed not to be sure of himself, as if he had got into the wrong house. He was a large man, bonily built, with a heavy head covered by a hard derby, which he made no attempt to remove. His eyes seemed sad, but his lips, above which he wore a slight mustache, sought to smile; he was not otherwise prepossessing. The cuffs of his sleeves, Manischevitz noted, were frayed to the lining, and the dark suit was badly fitted. He had very large feet. Recovering from his fright, Manischevitz guessed he had left the door open and was being visited by a case worker from the Welfare Department—some came at night—for he had recently applied for welfare. Therefore he lowered himself into a chair opposite the Negro, trying, before the man's uncertain smile, to feel comfortable. The former tailor sat stiffly but patiently at the table, waiting for the investigator to take out his pad and pencil and begin asking questions; but before long he became convinced the man intended to do nothing of the sort.

"Who are you?" Manischevitz at last asked uneasily.

"If I may, insofar as one is able to, identify myself, I bear the name of Alexander Levine."

In spite of his troubles Manischevitz felt a smile growing on his lips. "You said Levine?" he politely inquired.

The Negro nodded. "That is exactly right."

Carrying the jest further, Manischevitz asked, "You are maybe Jewish?"

"All my life I was, willingly."

The tailor hesitated. He had heard of black Jews but had never met one. It gave an unusual sensation.

Recognizing in afterthought something odd about the tense of Levine's remark, he said doubtfully, "You ain't Jewish any more?"

Levine at this point removed his hat, revealing a very white part in his black hair, but quickly replaced it. He replied, "I have recently been disincarnated into an angel. As such, I offer you my humble assistance, if to offer is within my province and power—in the best sense." He lowered his eyes in apology. "Which calls for added explanation: I am what I am granted to be, and at present the completion is in the future."

"What kind of angel is this?" Manischevitz gravely asked.

"A bona fide angel of God, within prescribed limitations," answered Levine, "not to be confused with the members of any particular sect, order, or organization here on earth operating under a similar name."

Manischevitz was thoroughly disturbed. He had been expecting something, but not this. What sort of mockery was it—provided that Levine was an angel—of a faithful servant who had from childhood lived in the synagogues, concerned with the word of God?

To test Levine he asked, "Then where are your wings?"

The Negro blushed as well as he could. Manischevitz understood this from his altered expression. "Under certain circumstances we lose privileges and prerogatives upon returning to earth, no matter for what purpose or endeavoring to assist whomsoever."

"So tell me," Manischevitz said triumphantly, "how did you get here?"

"I was translated."

Still troubled, the tailor said, "If you are a Jew, say the blessing for bread."

Levine recited it in sonorous Hebrew.

Although moved by the familiar words Manischevitz still felt doubt he was dealing with an angel.

"If you are an angel," he demanded somewhat angrily, "give me the proof."

Levine wet his lips. "Frankly, I cannot perform either miracles or near-miracles, due to the fact that I am in a condition of probation. How long that will persist or even consist depends on the outcome."

Manischevitz racked his brains for some means of causing Levine positively to reveal his true identity, when the Negro spoke again:

"It was given me to understand that both your wife and you require assistance of a salubrious nature?"

The tailor could not rid himself of the feeling that he was the butt of a jokester. Is this what a Jewish angel looks like? he asked himself. This I am not convinced.

He asked a last question. "So if God sends to me an angel, why a black? Why not a white that there are so many of them?"

"It was my turn to go next," Levine explained.

Manischevitz could not be persuaded. "I think you are a faker."

Levine slowly rose. His eyes indicated disappointment and worry. "Mr. Manischevitz," he said tonelessly, "if you should desire me to be of assistance to you any time in the near future, or possibly before, I can be found"—he glanced at his fingernails—"in Harlem."

He was by then gone.

THE NEXT DAY Manischevitz felt some relief from his backache and was able to work four hours at pressing. The day after, he put in six hours; and the third day four again. Fanny sat up a little and asked for some halvah to suck. But after the fourth day the stabbing, breaking ache afflicted his back, and Fanny again lay supine, breathing with blue-lipped difficulty.

Manischevitz was profoundly disappointed at the return of his active pain and suffering. He had hoped for a longer interval of easement, long enough to have a thought other than of himself and his troubles. Day by day, minute after minute, he lived in pain, pain his only memory, questioning the necessity of it, inveighing, though with affection, against

God. Why *so much*, Gottenyu? If He wanted to teach His servant a lesson for some reason, some cause—the nature of His nature—to teach him, say, for reasons of his weakness, his pride, perhaps, during his years of prosperity, his frequent neglect of God—to give him a little lesson, why then any of the tragedies that had happened to him, any one would have sufficed to chasten him. But *all together*—the loss of both his children, his means of livelihood, Fanny's health and his—that was too much to ask one frail-boned man to endure. Who, after all, was Manischevitz that he had been given so much to suffer? A tailor. Certainly not a man of talent. Upon him suffering was largely wasted. It went nowhere, into nothing: into more suffering. His pain did not earn him bread, nor fill the cracks in the wall, nor lift, in the middle of the night, the kitchen table; only lay upon him, sleepless, so sharply oppressive that he could many times have cried out yet not heard himself this misery.

In this mood he gave no thought to Mr. Alexander Levine, but at moments when the pain wavered, slightly diminishing, he sometimes wondered if he had been mistaken to dismiss him. A black Jew and angel to boot—very hard to believe, but suppose he *had* been sent to succor him, and he, Manischevitz, was in his blindness too blind to understand? It was this thought that put him on the knife-point of agony.

Therefore the tailor, after much self-questioning and continuing doubt, decided he would seek the self-styled angel in Harlem. Of course he had great difficulty because he had not asked for specific directions, and movement was tedious to him. The subway took him to 116th Street, and from there he wandered in the open dark world. It was vast and its lights lit nothing. Everywhere were shadows, often moving. Manischevitz hobbled along with the aid of a cane, and not knowing where to seek in the blackened tenement buildings, would look fruitlessly through store windows. In the stores he saw people and everybody was black. It was an amazing thing to observe. When he was too tired, too unhappy to go farther, Manischevitz stopped in front of a tailor's shop. Out of familiarity with the appearance of it, with some sadness he entered. The tailor, an old skinny man with a mop of woolly gray hair, was sitting cross-legged on his workbench, sewing a pair of tuxedo pants that had a razor slit all the way down the seat.

"You'll excuse me, please, gentleman," said Manischevitz, admiring the tailor's deft thimbled fingerwork, "but you know maybe somebody by the name Alexander Levine?"

The tailor, who, Manischevitz thought, seemed a little antagonistic to him, scratched his scalp.

"Cain't say I ever heared dat name."

"Alex-ander Lev-ine," Manischevitz repeated it.

The man shook his head. "Cain't say I heared."

Manischevitz remembered to say: "He is an angel, maybe."

"Oh *him*," said the tailor, clucking. "He hang out in dat honky-tonk down here a ways." He pointed with his skinny finger and returned to sewing the pants.

Manischevitz crossed the street against a red light and was almost run down by a taxi. On the block after the next, the sixth store from the corner was a cabaret, and the name in sparkling lights was BELLA'S. Ashamed to go in, Manischevitz gazed through the neon-lit window, and when the dancing couples had parted and drifted away, he discovered at a table on the side, toward the rear, Alexander Levine.

He was sitting alone, a cigarette butt hanging from the corner of his mouth, playing solitaire with a dirty pack of cards, and Manischevitz felt a touch of pity for him, because Levine had deteriorated in appearance. His derby hat was dented and had a gray smudge. His ill-fitting suit was shabbier, as if he had been sleeping in it. His shoes and trouser cuffs were muddy, and his face covered with an impenetrable stubble the color of licorice. Manischevitz, though deeply disappointed, was about to enter, when a big-breasted Negress in a purple evening gown appeared before Levine's table, and with much laughter through many white teeth, broke into a vigorous shimmy. Levine looked at Manischevitz with a haunted expression, but the tailor was too paralyzed to move or acknowledge it. As Bella's gyrations continued Levine rose, his eyes lit in excitement. She embraced him with vigor, both his hands clasped around her restless buttocks, and they tangoed together across the floor, loudly applauded by the customers. She seemed to have lifted Levine off his feet and his large shoes hung limp as they danced. They slid past the windows where Manischevitz, white-faced, stood staring in. Levine winked slyly and the tailor left for home.

FANNY LAY AT death's door. Through shrunken lips she muttered concerning her childhood, the sorrows of the marriage bed, the loss of her children; yet wept to live. Manischevitz tried not to listen, but even without ears he would have heard. It was not a gift. The doctor panted up the stairs, a broad but bland, unshaven man (it was Sunday), and soon shook his head. A day at most, or two. He left at once to spare himself Manischevitz's multiplied sorrow; the man who never stopped hurting. He would someday get him into a public home.

Manischevitz visited a synagogue and there spoke to God, but God had absented himself. The tailor searched his heart and found no hope. When she died, he would live dead. He considered taking his life although he knew he wouldn't. Yet it was something to consider. Considering, you existed. He railed against God— Can you love a rock, a broom, an emptiness? Baring his chest, he smote the naked bones, cursing himself for having, beyond belief, believed.

Asleep in a chair that afternoon, he dreamed of Levine. He was standing before a faded mirror, preening small decaying opalescent wings. "This means," mumbled Manischevitz, as he broke out of sleep, "that it is possible he could be an angel." Begging a neighbor lady to look in on Fanny and occasionally wet her lips with water he drew on his thin coat, gripped his walking stick, exchanged some pennies for a subway token, and rode to Harlem. He knew this act was the last desperate one of his woe: to go seeking a black magician to restore his wife to invalidism. Yet if there was no choice, he did at least what was chosen.

He hobbled to Bella's, but the place seemed to have changed hands. It was now, as he breathed, a synagogue in a store. In the front, toward him, were several rows of empty wooden benches. In the rear stood the

Ark, its portals of rough wood covered with rainbows of sequins; under it a long table on which lay the sacred scroll unrolled, illuminated by the dim light from a bulb on a chain overhead. Around the table, as if frozen to it and the scroll, which they all touched with their fingers, sat four Negroes wearing skullcaps. Now as they read the Holy Word, Manischevitz could, through the plate-glass window, hear the singsong chant of their voices. One of them was old, with a gray beard. One was bubble-eyed. One was humpbacked. The fourth was a boy, no older than thirteen. Their heads moved in rhythmic swaying. Touched by this sight from his childhood and youth, Manischevitz entered and stood silent in the rear.

"Neshoma," said bubble eyes, pointing to the word with a stubby finger. "Now what dat mean?"

"That's the word that means soul," said the boy. He wore eyeglasses.

"Let's git on wid de commentary," said the old man.

"Ain't necessary," said the humpback. "Souls is immaterial substance. That's all. The soul is derived in that manner. The immateriality is derived from the substance, and they both, causally an' otherwise, derived from the soul. There can be no higher."

"That's the highest."

"Over de top."

"Wait a minute," said bubble eyes. "I don't see what is dat immaterial substance. How come de one gits hitched up to de odder?" He addressed the humpback.

"Ask me somethin' hard. Because it is substanceless immateriality. It couldn't be closer together, like all the parts of the body under one skin—closer."

"Hear now," said the old man.

"All you done is switched de words."

"It's the primum mobile, the substanceless substance from which comes all things that were incepted in the idea—you, me, and everything and body else."

"Now how did all dat happen? Make it sound simple."

"It de speerit," said the old man. "On de face of de water moved de speerit. An' dat was good. It say so in de Book. From de speerit ariz de man."

"But now listen here. How come it become substance if it all de time a spirit?"

"God alone done dat."

"Holy! Holy! Praise His Name."

"But has dis spirit got some kind of a shade or color?" asked bubble eyes, deadpan.

"Man, of course not. A spirit is a spirit."

"Then how come we is colored?" he said with a triumphant glare.

"Ain't got nothing to do wid dat."

"I still like to know."

"God put the spirit in all things," answered the boy. "He put it in the green leaves and the yellow flowers. He put it with the gold in the fishes and the blue in the sky. That's how come it came to us."

"Amen."

"Praise Lawd and utter loud His speechless Name."

"Blow de bugle till it bust the sky."

They fell silent, intent upon the next word. Manischevitz, with doubt, approached them.

"You'll excuse me," he said. "I am looking for Alexander Levine. You know him maybe?"

"That's the angel," said the boy.

"Oh *him*," snuffed bubble eyes.

"You'll find him at Bella's. It's the establishment right down the street," the humpback said.

Manischevitz said he was sorry that he could not stay, thanked them, and limped across the street. It was already night. The city was dark and he could barely find his way.

But Bella's was bursting with jazz and the blues. Through the window Manischevitz recognized the dancing crowd and among them sought Levine. He was sitting loose-lipped at Bella's side table. They were tippling from an almost empty whiskey fifth. Levine had shed his old clothes, wore a shiny new checkered suit, pearl-gray derby hat, cigar, and big, two-tone, button shoes. To the tailor's dismay, a drunken look had settled upon his formerly dignified face. He leaned toward Bella, tickled her earlobe with his pinky while whispering words that sent her into gales of raucous laughter. She fondled his knee.

Manischevitz, girding himself, pushed open the door and was not welcomed.

"This place reserved."

"Beat it, pale puss."

"Exit, Yankel, semitic trash."

But he moved toward the table where Levine sat, the crowd breaking before him as he hobbled forward.

"Mr. Levine," he spoke in a trembly voice. "Is here Manischevitz."

Levine glared blearily. "Speak yo' piece, son."

Manischevitz shivered. His back plagued him. Tremors tormented his legs. He looked around, everybody was all ears.

"You'll excuse me. I would like to talk to you in a private place."

"Speak, Ah is a private pusson."

Bella laughed piercingly. "Stop it, boy, you killin' me."

Manischevitz, no end disturbed, considered fleeing but Levine addressed him:

"Kindly state the pu'pose of yo' communication with yo's truly."

The tailor wet cracked lips. "You are Jewish. This I am sure."

Levine rose, nostrils flaring. "Anythin' else yo' got to say?"

Manischevitz's tongue lay like a slab of stone.

"Speak now or fo'ever hold off."

Tears blinded the tailor's eyes. Was ever man so tried? Should he say he believed a half-drunk Negro was an angel?

The silence slowly petrified.

Manischevitz was recalling scenes of his youth as a wheel in his mind whirred: believe, do not, yes, no, yes, no. The pointer pointed to yes, to between yes and no, to no, no it was yes. He sighed. It moved but one still had to make a choice.

"I think you are an angel from God." He said it in a broken voice, thinking, If you said it it was said. If you believed it you must say it. If you believed, you believed.

The hush broke. Everybody talked but the music began and they went on dancing. Bella, grown bored, picked up the cards and dealt herself a hand.

Levine burst into tears. "How you have humiliated me."

Manischevitz apologized.

"Wait'll I freshen up." Levine went to the men's room and returned in his old suit.

No one said good-bye as they left.

They rode to the flat via subway. As they walked up the stairs Manischevitz pointed with his cane at his door.

"That's all been taken care of," Levine said. "You go in while I take off."

Disappointed that it was so soon over, but torn by curiosity, Manischevitz followed the angel up three flights to the roof. When he got there the door was already padlocked.

Luckily he could see through a small broken window. He heard an odd noise, as though of a whirring of wings, and when he strained for a wider view, could have sworn he saw a dark figure borne aloft on a pair of strong black wings.

A feather drifted down. Manischevitz gasped as it turned white, but it was only snowing.

He rushed downstairs. In the flat Fanny wielded a dust mop under the bed, and then upon the cobwebs on the wall.

"A wonderful thing, Fanny," Manischevitz said. "Believe me, there are Jews everywhere."

Francine Prose

FAITH

from

Household Saints

THERESA KNEW HOW things appeared from the outside: Her family had committed her to a nuthouse. But by then, the only outside that mattered to her was the physical surface of things—the polish of the stone, the clean windowpane, the heavy ceramic dishes, so netted with hairline cracks that they'd turned the mottled gray-green of an Oriental brush painting. Pushing the scrub brush over the floor, she thought of how God had created that soap, that water. She saw the miracle in the granite, in the hard bright transparency of glass. The pattern in the netted china was as clear to her as a stenciled rose. She did not have to remind herself of these things, nor did she have to convince herself that Sister Cupertino was extraordinarily beautiful, as dear and familiar to her as her mother and father.

When she walked into Sister Cupertino's office, four mornings a week, the nun's wide face shone at her like the full moon, a flat white disc of light. Sister Cupertino interrogated her with pointless questions—what difference did it make when she had first learned to use the toilet? But always Theresa thought, without trying, of a story she had read:

A bishop visits an island on which he finds three hermits. While praying with them, he discovers that the hermits are saying the Lord's Prayer incorrectly and, despite their considerable slowness, finally teaches them to say it right. He bids them good-bye, sails away, and that night sees a light approaching him over the water. As the light grows brighter, he sees that it is the three hermits, skimming toward him, flying hand in hand over the sea.

"Father," they beg him, "tell us the Lord's Prayer again, we can't seem to get it right." And the bishop can only say,

"Brothers, pray for us."

It was obvious to Theresa that, like the hermits, Sister Cupertino was praising God in her own way, and that all her silly questions comprised some private Lord's Prayer. And so she repeated her own story (not out of any desire to help herself, she didn't need help) but rather as a gift—for Sister Cupertino and, of course, for God. It was a simple story, as Theresa told it: The letter from Fatima. The Little Flower. The Carmelites. College. Leonard. An ironing board, a visit from Jesus, an infinity of red-and-white-checked shirts. Invariably, Sister Cupertino would break in at this point, saying,

"Theresa, the laundry is only the laundry."

In an effort to convince Theresa of this, her occupational therapy was shifted to the hospital laundry, where she was put to work folding sheets. When Theresa first touched the heavy institutional cotton (washed smoother than the finest percale), she nearly cried out with joy. She learned to fold each sheet with four swift motions, always the same four, stretching and snapping her arms with such precision and concentration that the sheets came out in identical rectangles—straight edges and perfect corners. Occasionally her rhythm was broken by a torn or stained sheet which had to be sorted out; the rips and spots were as precious to her as the blood on Jesus' shroud.

The laundry was hot and steamy, the smell of detergent intoxicating, and Jesus was there. Theresa felt His warmth in the sheets fresh from the dryer; the soft hospital cotton was the touch of His hand in hers. He was closer to her than the width of Leonard's ironing board, and she was folding the sheets for Him.

WHAT MADE ALL this bearable for Joseph and Catherine was their faith that it was only temporary. Convinced that each musty train ride was bringing them closer to the last one they would ever have to take, they almost began to enjoy them. They ordered their weeks around these Sunday trips and prepared for them as if for important journeys. Joseph purchased an accordion grate to pull across the storefront on Saturday nights. Catherine bought him a pair of driving gloves with pigskin palms, and it pleased them both to see these elegant gloves hailing taxis in the rain. Catherine learned to recognize the regulars, other passengers with relatives at Stella Maris. Although they avoided each other's eyes and never spoke, they formed a kind of family—no more distant and no less connected than the Falconettis.

Their visits took place in the solarium, where Theresa served them tea in paper cups and seemed quite fascinated by news of Joseph's business, Catherine's neighborhood gossip. If this were the Carmelite convent, thought Joseph, there would be no gossip, no tea.

Eventually, what they minded most about these trips was the weather. Every Sunday, it rained or sleeted or snowed. The train was always too hot or too cold, so damp and smelly that Catherine felt queasy. Yet even this discomfort came to seem reassuring; even the bad weather was dependable, and this dependability was what they liked about Stella Maris. They knew approximately where they would find Theresa, knew what she would be doing and how she would look. Each Sunday, Catherine took a deep breath and told herself that the other shoe had finally dropped: There were no more surprises.

And so they were doubly surprised when they arrived on a rainy Sunday afternoon in early May and were told that Theresa was resting in her room.

"Something's wrong," said Catherine. "I knew it the minute I got up this morning."

All that was wrong was a slight touch of the flu—nothing serious, according to the nuns who padded in and out on their gum-soled shoes, bringing aspirin and orange juice. Doctor Fontana had been in to check on her that morning and had prescribed an antibiotic. With God's help she would recover in three or four days.

Theresa didn't even look sick. She was wearing the sort of washed-out white flannel nightgown which can make healthy people look deathly ill; even so, her color was good, almost too good for a girl who'd spent the winter shuttling between an overheated laundry and a cold stone floor. Propped up on pillows, she lay between crisp sheets, her hands folded over the rough green blanket.

"At least it got her out of the laundry," whispered Joseph.

"Shh." Catherine hurried to give Theresa a hug and kiss. Joseph held back.

"You contagious?" he said. "I've got to go to work tomorrow."

"Papa." Theresa patted the edge of the bed. "Come sit by me. I need your help."

"At your service." Joseph took off his driving gloves and rubbed his hands together, blowing into his palms. "What can I do for you?"

"I need some advice."

Joseph looked at Catherine. He couldn't remember Theresa ever asking him for advice. Maybe Stella Maris was doing her good.

"What about?"

"Pinochle," said Theresa.

"Pinochle?" Joseph laughed so hard that he had to sit down. "Is that what you're doing here with my money? Playing pinochle?"

"We don't play for money. Just points."

"That's a relief," said Joseph. "Who do you play with?"

"God the Father and Jesus and St. Therese."

Joseph laughed again, less heartily than before. "You mean, there's people here who think they're God and Jesus and—"

"I mean God and Jesus and St. Therese."

Joseph glanced at Catherine. She was patting the air: Easy, take it easy. Humor her.

"You folks play often?" he asked.

"Last night was the first time. God had to teach me the rules. Of course they let me have a few practice hands. But you would have been proud of me, Papa. I got the hang of it right away."

"It's in the blood," said Joseph.

Catherine groaned.

"Don't worry, Mama. If God's playing, it's got to be all right."

"This is crazy," said Joseph. "This is the craziest thing I ever heard."

Catherine shot him a warning look.

"You play partners?" he said.

"Girls against boys."

"I should have known," said Joseph.

"We got slaughtered, Papa. We never had a chance. Please don't tell anyone I said so, but the Little Flower wasn't much of a pinochle player. She mumbled so low you couldn't hear what she bid. God had to make her repeat herself twenty times. It seemed like she passed them every card they needed—it was like she didn't want to win."

"That's a saint for you," said Catherine.

"I guess." Theresa sighed. "I guess I'll never be a saint. I wanted to win, I played hard. But even if I'd been an expert . . . we still didn't have a chance. Because God and Jesus drew nothing but high cards—straights, flushes, the jack of diamonds, the queen of spades. Between them, they controlled every hand. We quit when they had five hundred points and St. Therese and I had zero."

"Honey," said Catherine, "it was God you were playing with. Wouldn't you expect Him to win?"

"You too?" Joseph stared at her.

"I never expected to be playing pinochle with God," said Theresa.

"I know what you mean," admitted Catherine.

"And if I had," continued Theresa, "I would have expected Him to play fair."

"He didn't?"

Theresa looked around the room and out into the hall, as if to make sure that no one was listening.

"If it hadn't been God, I would have sworn he was cheating."

"He probably was," said Joseph.

"He was." Again Theresa checked for eavesdroppers. "After the game was over, God let the others leave before Him. On His way out, He stopped and whispered real low so the others couldn't hear:

" 'Theresa,' He told me, 'of all my great miracles, my favorites are tipping the scales and cheating at pinochle.' "

"That's what He said. Can you believe it?"

"I can believe it." Joseph looked pale.

No one spoke for a long time. Then Catherine said,

"Joseph, what time have you got?"

Joseph looked at his watch.

"The four-o'clock train left ten minutes ago. We'd better go, we'll be stuck at the station all night."

"We'll call tomorrow," said Catherine. "You rest up, and get better."

"I feel wonderful," said Theresa. "Don't worry."

Catherine touched her forehead.

"You're burning up. I'll send the nurse in when we go."

Joseph and Catherine kissed their daughter's flushed face and left. They were silent in the taxi, but in the train Joseph said,

"It's happening again. All that money we paid, and it's happening again."

"Nothing's happening," said Catherine. "She's had a fever. She was delirious."

"That's nothing? Anyhow, I don't believe that's it. What about the last time, at Leonard's. Ninety-eight-point-six."

"This is different. You heard the nurses. In three or four days, she'll be fine."

They watched the landscape rush by, rain pecking holes in the melting snow.

"This has got to be some kind of record," said Joseph. "Snow in May." Then he said,

"Listen, how much did she know?"

"About what?"

"You know about what. The pinochle game. Before we got married."

"Maybe she knew, maybe not. *I* didn't tell her. But people talk. . . . What difference does it make?"

"It seems like the end of the story," said Joseph. "Twenty years ago, I won my wife in a card game. And now our crazy daughter is playing pinochle with God."

"Take it easy. It's not your fault. No one ever went crazy because her father won her mother in a pinochle game."

"I'm not saying it's my fault. Far from it. I'm saying there's a pattern."

"Patterns. Next you'll be counting potato eyes like your mother."

"Look at that rain," said Joseph, and that was the end of the conversation till the train was pulling into Penn Station. Then Joseph turned to Catherine and said,

"It makes you think. I mean, maybe there is a God, and He's the kind of guy who cheats at pinochle. Isn't that what they say, that you make Him in your own image? And like your father says: Isn't it perfect? Isn't it just perfect that a God who cheats at pinochle would end the story this way?"

BUT IT WASN'T the end of the story.

There was something which Catherine never told Joseph. Ordinarily she might have mentioned it, but his talk on the train about patterns made her keep it to herself:

Every Sunday evening, they had sausage fried with onions and peppers. Easy, quick, delicious, it was by now an integral part of their weekly ritual. But that Sunday, Theresa's illness had so altered their established routine that Catherine couldn't even fry the sausage without feeling that something was different.

She was almost finished cooking when she realized that one of her cacti had flowered—the one she'd bought at Woolworth's on that morning when Theresa disappeared. In all the years since, it had neither grown nor shrunk, blossomed nor looked any less like a pebble than it did that first day. Still Catherine had gone on watering it, treasuring it as a kind of memento which she could no more throw away than she could Theresa's baby pictures.

Now there was a marble-sized lump on top, covered with downy spines, a dark red tinged with fuchsia, like the center of a rose.

Catherine had always loved flowering plants. But this one terrified her, and she moved it to the back of the shelf where she wouldn't have to see it. This unaccountable dread stayed with her all night and woke her at five in the morning, thinking: There's more. The other shoe.

When the phone rang, she was not even startled, but lay there patiently, waiting for Joseph to answer.

"Mister Santangelo," said the voice on the phone, "this is Sister Cupertino from Stella Maris. I'm sorry to call so early, but I have some bad news for you. Mister Santangelo, your daughter has gone to God."

"Gone where?" Joseph mumbled groggily.

"To heaven."

"No," said Joseph.

"What's wrong?" said Catherine. "What happened?"

"Mister Santangelo, are you still there?"

"I'm here. What happened?"

"God took her."

"I mean how. How did it happen?"

"What?" said Catherine. "Joseph, tell me."

"Fever," said Sister Cupertino. "A sudden high fever. That's all we know. Sister Lucy went in to check on her on her morning rounds at four. She took Theresa's temperature. It was a hundred and six. She went to call Doctor Fontana, and when she got back at four-fifteen, Theresa had passed away—"

"It took her fifteen minutes to make a phone call?"

"Mister Santangelo, it was four in the morning. She got the doctor's answering service. Believe me, it was a great shock to us all."

"We'll be right out." Joseph hung up the phone.

"Theresa's dead," said Catherine.

Joseph put his arms around her and they held each other without speaking until Catherine said,

"I feel like a hole's opened up in the world and my life's fallen through."

"I know what you mean," said Joseph. "About the hole." They got up and got dressed.

"I guess there's no hurry," said Joseph. "We might as well wait for the light to come up." They drank coffee till shortly after dawn, then left.

It was a clear spring morning, so lovely that it seemed a shame to sleep it away, and Mulberry Street was wide awake. Shopkeepers were hosing down the sidewalk in front of their stores. Rainbows shone in the spray, and the asphalt gleamed in the morning sun. Early as it was, the streets were full of people dressed for work—secretaries in the new spring dresses which they'd bought as promises to themselves in the middle of winter.

"Wouldn't you know it?" said Joseph. "Now's when we get a good day for traveling."

Catherine stared at him.

"Some good day," she said.

At the entrance to Penn Station, boys were selling bunches of daffodils.

"You want some flowers?" asked Joseph.

"Daffodils? What for?"

As the train rolled through the suburbs, Joseph and Catherine saw patches of green on every lawn. They passed freshly plowed gardens, and the air carried the smell of manure. Half the trees were surrounded by the reddish aura which immediately precedes the formation of buds; the other half were already in bud.

"You know at the end of 'Red Riding Hood'?" said Catherine. "When they cut the wolf's stomach open and fill it with stones? That's how my stomach feels."

"Red Riding Hood?" murmured Joseph. He pointed out the window. "What's that?"

"I don't know. A hyacinth, maybe."

In the taxi, Catherine said,

"In the sunshine, it's a whole different ride."

Stella Maris looked so unfamiliar that Catherine was momentarily afraid that the cab driver had let them off at the wrong place.

"Jesus," said Joseph. "Would you look at that?"

"I'm looking," said Catherine.

The garden was in full bloom. Delicate pink strands hung from the weeping cherries like the fringes of a shawl. The forsythia and early willow were bright yellow, the new grass yellow-green. Beds of daffodils, violets and blue forget-me-nots lined the walkway, and sunlight shone pearly and translucent through drifts of jonquils.

"It's not natural," whispered Joseph.

"What? What are you whispering for?"

"It's not natural. It's not right. Yesterday it was winter and today it's spring."

"Some years it happens like that."

"Not like this. Mud one day, the next a garden. Besides, you saw on the way out—the rest of the Island doesn't look like this."

"They've got good gardeners. The Church always gets the best. There's always some monsignor who'll throw a fit if he sees a dandelion on the lawn."

"The *Pope* couldn't do this. Not overnight."

"What do you know about it? The closest you ever got to nature was Frank Manzone's vegetable stand."

"Enough to know that you don't pull a garden out of a hat."

"It's not out of a hat. There were buds yesterday, the flowers were ready to pop. But it was raining, you didn't notice. . . ."

"Believe me, I would have noticed."

"But you didn't."

"Okay, you're the plant lady. You tell me. Is this natural or not?"

Joseph had stopped beside a bed of daffodils and was looking down at the flowers. They were all the same color: creamy white, with pale yellow centers and saffron stigmata. Joseph wanted to touch the orange stamens, but hesitated. Strangely, he was remembering his wedding night—how scared he'd been to touch Catherine. That night, he'd convinced himself that it was not just permissible—but necessary for life to go on. Yet now, nothing could have persuaded him to touch the inside of those flowers.

"It's those patterns again," he said. "Even the weather's in on it. Remember how hot it was, the night of that pinochle game? And how it rained the next day when you came into the shop? Now for months it rains every Sunday and all of a sudden, the sun . . ."

"Joseph." Catherine spoke very softly. "Theresa's lying out here dead and we're talking about the weather."

"You think I forgot?" said Joseph. "What else should we talk about?"

Catherine had turned her back to him. Her head was bent, her shoulders rounded. Joseph had to remind himself that forty wasn't old, because at that moment the alley cat he had married looked like an old woman.

"I'm sorry," he said, then put his arm around her and kept it there till they reached the lobby.

Sister Cupertino and a priest whom she introduced as Father Dominic were waiting for them. Father Dominic was a thin little man with pointed features, blue-white skin, dark circles under his eyes and a heavy five-o'clock shadow. It occurred to Joseph that the priest looked worse than Theresa ever did, and Theresa was dead.

Sister Cupertino took Catherine's hands between her dry palms and held them. Father Dominic, whose hands were somewhat stickier, did the same to Joseph.

"Good morning." Father Dominic's voice was nearly expressionless, but the solemn look on his face said, God's will be done.

"That's some garden you got out there," said Joseph.

Sister Cupertino and Father Dominic exchanged knowing looks. They'd seen it before—so many families needed that small talk, that buffer before getting down to the tragic business at hand.

"Isn't it?" said Sister Cupertino. "After all the bad weather we've been having, it's a miracle."

Joseph gave her a funny look.

"It always come like that? Overnight?"

"Mister Santangelo, it's practically the middle of May."

Father Dominic ushered them to Theresa's room, then discreetly vanished. Joseph and Catherine hesitated in the doorway. But when they forced themselves inside, they saw that Theresa looked almost exactly as she had the day before—only paler, eyes shut. Her head was still propped up on pillows, her hands folded over the blanket.

"It's hard to believe," said Catherine.

"What's that smell?" said Joseph.

"What's got into you today?" Catherine sniffed. "I don't know, some kind of flowers."

"Roses," said Joseph. "It's enough to knock you over."

"So?"

"There's no roses in this room. Do you see roses in this room?"

"Calm down. Maybe one of the nurses was wearing perfume."

"You know nuns don't wear perfume."

"Then maybe an orderly. Maybe the doctor was wearing cologne."

"It's not cologne."

"Air freshener, then. How should I know?"

"No air freshener in the world smells like this."

"Maybe it's coming from the outside. From the garden."

Joseph went to the window.

"There's a parking lot out there." Beyond it, he saw green. . . . "It didn't smell like this *in* the garden."

"So they had flowers in here and took them out."

"Why would they do that? Besides, that smell that sticks around when you take flowers out of a room—it's always kind of stale. And this isn't stale, it's like going up to a rose and sticking your nose right in it."

Joseph approached the bed.

"It's coming from Theresa. Did you ever know her to use perfume?"

"Theresa?" Catherine came closer. "You're right. Maybe it's some kind of soap they use here."

"I know the smell of soap." Joseph shook his head.

Kneeling by the side of the bed, Catherine said a Hail Mary, and Our Father, then added her personal prayer that Theresa's soul would go straight to heaven. She imagined St. Peter greeting her at the gate, saying, "Theresa! How perfect that you should come today, it's spring cleaning!" And Theresa would enter paradise to find the angels sweeping the clouds with golden brooms, raising puffs of feathery dust.

When Catherine stood, Joseph said,

"It's not natural for a healthy young girl to die in one night with no warning."

"I thought they told you it was fever."

"Fever? What do psychiatrists know about fever?"

"So maybe it wasn't fever. Maybe it was her heart. Or some medicine they gave her. She's dead, what can we do now? What do you think, they murdered her? What do you want, revenge?"

"I guess God took her," said Joseph. "Like the lady said."

"Maybe so. We might as well think so."

"It doesn't help. It doesn't help at all."

"I know," said Catherine. Then Joseph said,

"Isn't that what's supposed to happen when a saint dies? Everything starts smelling like flowers?"

Catherine glanced at him. Was he joking? But he was serious when he said,

"Suppose she was one."

"A saint? Theresa?"

"Sure, why not? Maybe she got what she wanted."

"Joseph, Theresa was a beautiful girl. A good girl. I'll never love anyone in my life like I loved her. But she was crazy, Joseph. She went crazy ironing shirts in her boyfriend's apartment."

"Saints have done crazier. Look. Look at this." Joseph held up Theresa's hands. Not yet rigid, they bent gracefully at the wrists—both of which were covered with a network of red lines, faintly streaked with blood.

"What's this? Catherine, what's this?"

"What do you think? Stigmata?"

"What then?"

"Mosquito bites. She scratched herself in her sleep."

"Mosquitoes in May?"

"Sure, in May."

"Catherine, remember how much she used to pray? All those times she fasted. Who else acts like that but a saint? Suppose that's what she was?"

"A saint?"

"Who knows? There's been miracles here. First the garden, then that smell in the room, the stigmata, even the way she died . . ."

"You're upset. You're letting it get to you. There haven't been any miracles. Nothing's happened, nothing ever happened to us that couldn't happen normally. The garden was green yesterday—you just didn't notice. Theresa could have started wearing perfume here at the hospital—how would we know? Yesterday she was dying and we didn't even see it. Maybe the burning bush was burning all the time and Moses didn't notice. Maybe the miracle is when you stop and pay attention."

"I don't get it," said Joseph.

"We're not talking about walking on water," said Catherine. "We're talking about ordinary life. Remember when I thought that the dead plants in our place had been resurrected and the truth was, you'd watered them and bought new ones? Remember how your mother thought it was a miracle when that geranium bloomed on the mantelpiece—and all the time I'd known it was going to?"

"It flowered." Joseph was thinking of the daffodil bed. "No matter who knew. Maybe *that* was the miracle."

"Maybe so. But it's not the kind of thing they canonize you for." Again Catherine sniffed the air. The smell was getting stronger. "So what if it is a miracle? What then?"

"Somebody should be told. Someone in the church . . ."

"The church? You must be kidding."

"It's what Theresa would have wanted."

"Okay, that's it." Catherine dusted her palms together. "Forget it, just forget it. There's arrangements to make."

Sister Cupertino—her manner so breezy that she might have been outlining another phase of Theresa's treatment—served them coffee in her office while discussing the funeral arrangements. When at last the Santangelos rose to leave, she put her doughy arms around their shoulders, smiled ruefully and said,

"If Theresa had lived in another era, they might have called her a saint."

"If they'd had lithium in Jesus' time," said Joseph, "there wouldn't have been any saints."

"Joseph," said Catherine, "let's go."

"If they'd had mental hospitals, they'd have had John the Baptist on occupational therapy," muttered Joseph, and that was the last that either of them spoke till they were nearly home. Finally Catherine said,

"Joseph, it's not as if I believe this. But suppose Theresa was a saint—miracles, stigmata, the works. What if we told somebody and they took us seriously, and the church just happened to need an *American* Little Flower of Jesus? Service and devotion in every little thing—even ironing shirts in a Catholic law student's apartment. Then what? Then poor Theresa, that's what. Would you want her to spend eternity like that, people lighting candles—"

"Who lights candles anymore?"

"There will always be somebody. Telling the saints their problems, begging them for help they can't give. Is that what you want for your daughter? Hasn't she done enough favors?"

"I never thought of it that way," said Joseph.

Catherine waited till they were back in the apartment, then closed and locked the door.

"Joseph," she said, "if you really think that Theresa was a saint, if you think we've seen miracles—think what you want, but keep your mouth shut. For Theresa's sake, Joseph, if you ever loved her—don't tell a soul."

ONE FOOT IN front of the other: This was what was meant by God's mercy. It seemed to Catherine as if her body were producing its own morphine, stronger than any painkiller a doctor could prescribe. She wasn't expected to do anything, and yet she was so numb that she could help Joseph hang the bunting and accept her neighbors' condolences without bursting into tears. The only trouble with this wonder drug was that it tended to wear off in the middle of the night. And it disappeared completely when she and Joseph walked into the funeral parlor and saw all the roses.

The night after Theresa died had been the first warm evening of spring. The old people had dusted off their folding chairs and come out to take the air, to thank God for the weather and to remark how strange it was that they were alive to enjoy this breeze when a twenty-year-old girl lay dead. At this, the grandmothers had picked at their stockings and waited for their husbands to tease them out of their misery. But their husbands were in no mood for teasing. A young person's death was always a tragedy—but this was like losing a daughter.

It wasn't that they'd felt particularly close to Theresa. She'd kept to herself, they hadn't loved her as they'd loved their children's friends, their grandchildren's friends, the neighbors' kids they'd fed and hugged and practically adopted. But they knew where Theresa came from, and her story was part of them, absorbed into their systems with every sausage they'd eaten in the last thirty years. The old people remembered Mrs. Santangelo and were shocked to realize how long she'd been gone. Middle-aged couples remembered being young and single and dancing at the wedding of the man who'd won his wife at a card game. The women remembered when their children were young and they'd traded stories with Catherine. Now their Mary Kay was married, their Sal had a good job in the garment district, and Theresa was dead.

Her story had marked off their lives, become part of their own life stories—they couldn't stand to know that it was ending this way. Only the good die young, they said so often that they couldn't think of Theresa without conjuring up one of those marble lambs curled up on an infant's tombstone.

Individually and together, the Santangelos' neighbors came to the same conclusion. The only appropriate gesture—the only way to honor such innocence, to sweeten such a bitter end—was to spare no expense and send roses.

And so it happened that Joseph and Catherine walked into Castellano's Funeral Home to find every surface covered with roses—massed on the altar, down the steps, on trestle tables lining the side aisles and spilling from the windowsills so that all four walls were blanketed with roses.

Catherine began to cry. Joseph put his arms around her to support her, and caught himself leaning on her. People were looking at them, trying not to stare, but Joseph and Catherine were alone in that chapel with the roses and Theresa's body. Catherine prayed that Joseph wouldn't start talking about patterns again, because now she was seeing them too, and this one made her angry.

She was remembering her wedding, the feast which—like these roses—had appeared out of nowhere. Two miracles, two magic tricks, except that both times all Mulberry Street was in on it. Like the wedding guests, the mourners in the lobby looked as if they knew something she didn't, knew that it was more than her wedding, more than her daughter's funeral. And suddenly she felt as if her whole life had been planned this way, without consulting her, contrived to satisfy someone's idea of some old story which had nothing to do with her: First the wedding at Cana and now this shower of roses.

She got angrier each time an old woman filed by and laid a white rosary in the coffin. Nor did it help when Joseph whispered in her ear,

"You know who sent those roses? The same guy who stacked that pinochle deck."

All through the wake, the smell of roses grew stronger. By the funeral, their perfume was stale, almost suffocating. Joseph and Catherine barely heard the service; then someone ushered them into a black limousine. As the car swung through a complicated series of turns onto the highway, Joseph looked back and saw that the cortege was so long, every car in the cloverleaf behind them had its lights on.

Later, Catherine would remember nothing about the graveside except her fear that she would never stop crying. When the coffin was lowered, Joseph couldn't watch, and instead looked around and saw that no one could watch.

For the first time that anyone could remember, no one went back to the family's house after the service. Catherine had planned on having her neighbors in, but when she saw all the roses, she'd let it be known that she didn't want company.

By evening, the merciful numbness had returned and Catherine went to bed early. Joseph waited till she was asleep, then went out with Augie to get drunk at the San Remo, where he told his brother the whole story. Perhaps it was the wine, or the will to believe that his daughter's life had

had more meaning than a premature death in a nuthouse. Whatever the reason, Joseph heard himself talking as if Theresa were really a saint:

"You can tell me they were mosquito bites, but I say no. That hospital room smelled stronger than the funeral parlor this morning. And Augie, I swear to God: We were out there the day before, and that garden was dead. I keep seeing patterns—patterns in everything. Even that hot night, that night I won Catherine at pinochle—God was stacking the deck. God was turning up the heat."

Augie went home and told Evelyn. By noon the next day, the entire neighborhood had heard about the peculiar circumstances surrounding Theresa's death, and everyone was so happy to think that her story might have a different end that they were already beginning to revise it. Now suddenly people remembered that long-ago morning when Theresa got lost and was found splashing in the holy water. Former schoolmates recalled the ceremony in which she'd received *The Story of a Soul*. Except for some rumors about trouble with a boy, no one had much recent knowledge of the shy, stand-offish girl, and so it was easy to invent details.

Each teller added new examples of her charity, her obedience, her patience. Somehow the rumor got started that a string of miracles had followed soon upon her death. It was said that all the patients at Stella Maris recovered instantaneously on the day of Theresa's funeral and were discharged to make room for a new generation of residents. It was said that the hospital gardens retained their bloom all summer and were discovered to have healing powers; busloads of schizophrenics were imported from Pilgrim State and cured by touching Theresa's favorite rose trellis. It was said that her bereaved parents gave her radio to her grandfather, and that this radio would play nothing but religious stations, picked up from all over the country. It was said that Lino Falconetti made no attempt to fix the set, though he lived another ten years and died believing himself a lucky man.

Finally it was said that Theresa's holiness could still be partaken of by buying sausage from her father's shop. Following her death, it was rumored, Joseph Santangelo never cheated a customer again. There were many who knew for a fact that this was untrue, and they told it like this:

After the mourning period, Joseph reopened his shop and started cheating like never before. And when the women complained, he would flash them his sweetest smile and say, "You know who cheats? God cheats. Go complain to Him."

But by then, the facts of Theresa's life and death were less important than the story and the reasons people told it:

At school, the good girls told it as conclusive proof that it was still possible to lead a consecrated life: God knew who thought good thoughts and helped around the house. At night, the men came home from playing cards and retold it, as if to say: You may think we're wasting our time playing cards, but for all you know—we're preparing the way for a saint. And their wives made similar claims whenever they ruined a meal, on those days when everything went wrong in the kitchen.

In the daytime, though, the women told it differently, to each other. The happy women, and the women who still imagined that happiness was attainable, sighed and said, "If only it would happen to me. If only I could see God in the dirty laundry." And the women who looked back on a lifetime of laundry and thought, What did I do it for? said, "Why bother? Look where it gets you—the nuthouse."

"What kind of life did she lead?" they said. "Nothing was accomplished, nothing left behind. She went crazy and died and went into the ground and that was it." Then the others would point out some little girl with a bag of groceries.

"Life goes on," they said, and the women would look at each other, not knowing how to feel.

The only ones who could tell the story with no mixed feelings and nothing to prove were the very old. They told it with reverence, with the same respect they would have shown the life of a saint. They told it as Theresa would have liked it told, as the story of an ordinary life redeemed by extraordinary devotion. They told it for hope, and its comfort stayed with them even as Theresa's life receded into that time when everything was bigger and better and more extreme.

They saved it for the hottest nights, when the air was so heavy that they couldn't breathe, so still that they could hear the untrustworthy rhythm of their heartbeats. They told it quietly, as if telling a bedtime story to a grandchild. But this was the story they told to reassure themselves, to remind each other:

Wait. Such things can happen to anyone, on any hot night—a hot night exactly like this. Hush. Listen to the sound of cards slapping on the table. God is sending us a saint.

Richard Bausch

Design

THE REVEREND TARMIGIAN was not well. You could see it in his face—a certain hollowness, a certain blueness in the skin. His eyes lacked luster and brightness. He had a persistent dry, deep cough; he'd lost a lot of weight. And yet on this fine, breezy October day he was out on the big lawn in front of his church, raking leaves. Father Russell watched him from the window of his study, and knew that if he didn't walk over there and say something to him about it, this morning—like so many recent mornings—would be spent fretting and worrying about Tarmigian, seventy-two years old and out raking leaves in the windy sun. He had been planning to speak to the old man for weeks, but what could you say to a man like that? An institution in Point Royal, old Tarmigian had been pastor of the neighboring church—Faith Baptist, only a hundred or so yards away on the other side of Tallawaw Creek—for more than three decades. He referred to himself in conversation as the

Reverend Fixture. He was a stooped, frail man with wrinkled blue eyes and fleecy blond hair that showed freckled scalp in the light; there were dimples in his cheeks. One of his favorite jokes—one of the many jokes he was fond of repeating—was that he had the eyes of a clown built above the natural curve of a baby's bottom. He'd touch the dimples and smile, saying a thing like that. And the truth was he tended to joke too much—even about the fact that he was apparently taxing himself beyond the dictates of good health for a man his age.

It seemed clear to Father Russell—who was all too often worried about his own health, though he was thirty years younger than Tarmigian—that something was driving the older man to these stunts of killing work: raking leaves all morning in the fall breezes; climbing on a ladder to clear drainspouts; or, as he had done one day last week, lugging a bag of mulch across the road and up the hill to the little cemetery where his wife lay buried, as if there weren't plenty of people within arm's reach on any Sunday who would have done it gladly for him (and would have just as gladly stood by while he said his few quiet prayers over the grave). His wife had been dead twenty years, he had the reverential respect of the whole countryside, but something was driving the man and, withal, there was often a species of amused cheerfulness about him almost like elation, as though he were keeping some wonderful secret.

It was perplexing; it violated all the rules of respect for one's own best interest. And today, watching him rake leaves, Father Russell determined that he would speak to him about it. He would simply confront him—broach the subject of health and express an opinion. Father Russell understood enough about himself to know that this concern would seem uncharacteristically personal on his part—it might even be misconstrued in some way—but as he put a jacket on and started out of his own church, it was with a small thrill of resolution. It was time to interfere, regardless of the age and regardless of the fact that it had been Father Russell's wish to find ways of avoiding the company of the older man.

Tarmigian's church was at the top of a long incline, across a stone bridge over Tallawaw Creek. It was a rigorous walk, even on a cool day, as this one was. The air was blue and cool in the mottled shade, and there were little patches of steam on the creek when the breezes were still. The Reverend Tarmigian stopped working, leaned on the handle of the rake and watched Father Russell cross the bridge.

"Well, just in time for coffee."

"I'll have tea," Father Russell said, a little out of breath from the walk.

"You're winded," said Tarmigian.

"And you're white as a sheet."

It was true. Poor Tarmigian's cheeks were pale as death. There were two blotches on them, like bruises—caused, Father Russell was sure, by the blood vessels that were straining to break in the old man's head. He indicated the trees all around, burnished-looking and still loaded with leaves, and even now dropping some of them, like part of an argument for the hopelessness of this task the old man had set for himself.

"Why don't you at least wait until they're finished?" Father Russell demanded.

"I admit, it's like emptying the ocean with a spoon." Tarmigian put his rake down and motioned for the other man to follow him. They went through the back door into the older man's tidy little kitchen, where Father Russell watched him fuss and worry, preparing the tea. When it was ready, the two men went into the study to sit among the books and talk. It was the old man's custom to take an hour every day in this book-lined room, though with this bad cold he'd contracted, he hadn't been up to much of anything recently. It was hard to maintain his old fond habits, he said. He felt too tired, or too sick. It was just an end-of-summer cold, of course, and Tarmigian dismissed it with a wave of his hand. Yet Father Russell had observed the weight loss, the coughing; and the old man was willing to admit that lately his appetite had suffered.

"I can't keep anything down," he said. "Sort of keeps me discouraged from trying, you know? So I shed the pounds. I'm sure when I get over this flu—"

"Medical science is advancing," said the priest, trying for sarcasm.

"They have doctors now with their own offices and instruments. It's all advanced to a sophisticated stage. You can even get medicine for the flu."

"I'm fine. There's no need for anyone to worry."

Father Russell had seen denial before: indeed, he saw some version of it almost every day, and he had a rich understanding of the psychology of it. Yet Tarmigian's statement caused a surprising little clot of anger to form in the back of his mind and left him feeling vaguely disoriented, as if the older man's blithe neglect of himself were a kind of personal affront.

Yet he found, too, that he couldn't come right out and say what he had come to believe: that the old man was jeopardizing his own health. The words wouldn't form on his lips. So he drank his tea and searched for an opening—a way of getting something across about learning to relax a bit, learning to take it easy. There wasn't a lot to talk about beyond Tarmigian's anecdotes and chatter. The two men were not particularly close: Father Russell had come to his own parish from Boston only a year ago, believing this small Virginia township to be the accidental equivalent of a demotion (the assignment, coming really like the drawing of a ticket out of a hat, was less than satisfactory). He had felt almost immediately that the overfriendly, elderly clergyman next door was a bit too southern for his taste—though Tarmigian was obviously a man of broad experience, having served in missions overseas as a young man, and it was true that he possessed a kind of simple, happy grace. So while the priest had spent a lot of time in the first days trying to avoid him for fear of hurting his feelings, he had learned finally that Tarmigian was unavoidable, and had come to accept him as one of the mild irritations of the place in which he now found himself. He had even considered that the man had a kind of charm, was amusing and generous. He would admit that there had been times when he found himself surprised by a faint stir of gladness when the old man could be seen on the little crossing bridge, heading down to pay another of his casual visits as if there were nothing better to do than to sit in Father Russell's parlor and make jokes about himself.

The trouble now, of course, was that everything about the old man, including his jokes, seemed tinged with the something terrible that the priest feared was happening to him. And here Father Russell was, watching him cough, watching him hold up one hand as if to ward off anything in the way of advice or concern about it. The cough took him deep, so that he had to gasp to get his breath back; but then he cleared his throat, sipped more of the tea and, looking almost frightfully white around the eyes, smiled and said, “I have a good one for you, Reverend Russell. I had a couple in my congregation—I won't name them, of course—who came to me yesterday afternoon, claiming they were going to seek a divorce. You know how long they've been married? They've been married fifty-two years. Fifty-two years and they say they can't stand each other. I mean can't stand to be in the same room with each other.”

Father Russell was interested in spite of himself—and in spite of the fact that the old man had again called him “Reverend.” This would be another of Tarmigian's stories, or another of his jokes. The priest felt the need to head him off. “That cough,” he said.

Tarmigian looked at him as if he'd merely said a number or recited a day's date.

“I think you should see a doctor about it.”

“It's just a cold, Reverend.”

“I don't mean to meddle,” said the priest.

“Yes, well. I was asking what you thought about a married couple can't stand to be in the same room together after fifty-two years.”

Father Russell said, “I guess I'd have to say I have trouble believing that.”

“Well, believe it. And you know what I said to them? I said we'd talk about it for a while. Counseling, you know.”

Father Russell said nothing.

“Of course,” said Tarmigian, “as you know, we permit divorce. Something about an English king wanting one badly enough to start his own church. Oh, that was long ago, of course. But we do allow it when it seems called for.”

“Yes,” Father Russell said, feeling beaten.

"You know, I don't think it's a question of either one of them being interested in anybody else. There doesn't seem to be any romance or anything—nobody's swept anybody off anybody's feet."

The priest waited for him to go on.

"I can't help feeling it's a bit silly." Tarmigian smiled, sipped the tea, then put the cup down and leaned back, clasping his hands behind his head. "Fifty-two years of marriage, and they want to untie the knot. What do you say, shall I send them over to you?"

The priest couldn't keep the sullen tone out of his voice. "I wouldn't know what to say to them."

"Well—you'd tell them to love one another. You'd tell them that love is the very breath of living or some such thing. Just as I did."

Father Russell muttered, "That's what I'd have to tell them, of course."

Tarmigian smiled again. "We concur."

"What was their answer?"

"They were going to think about it. Give themselves some time to think, really. That's no joke, either." Tarmigian laughed, coughing. Then it was just coughing.

"That's a terrible cough," said the priest, feeling futile and afraid and deeply irritable. His own words sounded to him like something learned by rote.

"You know what I think I'll tell them if they come back?"

He waited.

"I think I'll tell them to stick it out anyway, with each other." Tarmigian looked at him and smiled. "Have you ever heard anything more absurd?"

Father Russell made a gesture, a wave of the hand, that he hoped the other took for agreement.

Tarmigian went on: "It's probably exactly right—probably exactly what they should do, and yet such odd advice to think of giving two people who've been together fifty-two years. I mean, when do you think the phrase 'sticking it out' would stop being applicable?"

Father Russell shrugged and Tarmigian smiled, seemed to be awaiting some reaction.

"Very amusing," said Father Russell.

But the older man was coughing again.

From the beginning there had been things Tarmigian said and did which unnerved the priest. Father Russell was a man who could be undone by certain kinds of boisterousness, and there were matters of casual discourse he simply would never understand. Yet often enough over the several months of their association, he had entertained the suspicion that Tarmigian was harboring a bitterness, and that his occasional mockery of himself was some sort of reaction to it, if it wasn't in fact a way of releasing it.

Now Father Russell sipped his tea and looked away out the window. Leaves were flying in the wind. The road was in blue shade, and the shade moved. There were houses beyond the hill, but from here everything looked like a wilderness.

"Well," Tarmigian said, gaining control of himself. "Do you know what my poor old couple say is their major complaint? Their major complaint is they don't like the same TV programs. Now, can you imagine a thing like that?"

"Look," the priest blurted out. "I see you from my study window—you're—you don't get enough rest. I think you should see a doctor about that cough."

Tarmigian waved this away. "I'm fit as a fiddle, as they say. Really."

"If it's just a cold, you know," said Father Russell, giving up. "Of course—" He could think of nothing else to say.

"You worry too much," Tarmigian said. "You know, you've got bags under your eyes."

TRUE.

In the long nights Father Russell lay with a rosary tangled in his fingers and tried to pray, tried to stop his mind from playing tricks on him:

the matter of greatest faith was and had been for a very long time now that every twist or turn of his body held a symptom, every change signified the onset of disease. It was all waiting to happen to him, and the anticipation of it sapped him, made him weak and sick at heart. He had begun to see that his own old propensity for morbid anxiety about his health was worsening, and the daylight hours required all his courage. Frequently he thought of Tarmigian as though the old man were in some strange way a reflection of his secretly held, worst fear. He recalled the lovely sunny mornings of his first summer as a curate, when he was twenty-seven and fresh and the future was made of slow time. This was not a healthy kind of thinking. It was middle age, he knew. It was a kind of spiritual dryness he had been taught to recognize and contend with. Yet each morning his dazed wakening—from whatever fitful sleep the night had yielded him—was greeted with the pall of knowing that the aging pastor of the next-door church would be out in the open, performing some strenuous task as if he were in the bloom of health. When the younger man looked out the window, the mere sight of the other building was enough to make him sick with anxiety.

ON FRIDAY FATHER RUSSELL went to Saint Celia Hospital to attend to the needs of one of his older parishioners, who had broken her hip in a fall, and while he was there a nurse walked in and asked that he administer the sacrament of extreme unction to a man in the emergency room. He followed her down the hall and the stairs to the first floor, and while they walked she told him the man had suffered a heart attack, that he was already beyond help. She said this almost matter-of-factly, and Father Russell looked at the delicate curve of her ears, thinking about design. This was, of course, an odd thing to be contemplating at such a somber time, yet he cultivated the thought, strove to concentrate on it, gazing at the intricacy of the nurse's red-veined earlobe. Early in his priesthood, he had taught himself to make his mind settle on other things during moments requiring him to look upon sickness and death—he had worked to foster a healthy appreciation of, and attention to, insignificant things which were out of the province of questions of eternity and salvation and the common doom. It was what he had always managed as a protection against too clear a memory of certain daily horrors—images that could blow through him in the night like the very winds of fright and despair—and if over the years it had mostly worked, it had recently been in the process of failing him. Entering the crowded emergency room, he was concentrating on the whorls of a young woman's ear as an instrument for hearing, when he saw Tarmigian sitting in one of the chairs near the television, his hand wrapped in a bandage, his pallid face sunk over the pages of a magazine.

Tarmigian looked up, then smiled, held up the bandaged hand. There wasn't time for the two men to speak. Father Russell nodded at him and went on, following the nurse, feeling strangely precarious and weak. He looked back over his shoulder at Tarmigian, who had simply gone back to reading the magazine, and then he was attending to what the nurse had brought him to see: she pulled a curtain aside to reveal a gurney with two people on it—a man and a woman of roughly the same late middle age—the woman cradling the man's head in her arms and whispering something to him.

"Mrs. Simpson," the nurse said, "here's the priest."

Father Russell stood there while the woman regarded him. She was perhaps fifty-five, with iron-gray hair and small, round, wet eyes. "Mrs. Simpson," he said to her.

"He's my husband," she murmured, rising, letting the man's head down carefully. His eyes were open wide, as was his mouth. "My Jack. Oh, Jack. Jack."

Father Russell stepped forward and touched her shoulder, and she cried, staring down at her husband's face.

"He's gone," she said. "We were talking, you know. We were thinking about going down to see the kids. And he just put his head down. We were talking about how the kids never come to visit and we were going to surprise them."

"Mrs. Simpson," the nurse said, "would you like a sedative? Something to settle your nerves—"

This had the effect of convincing the poor woman about what had just taken place: the reality of it sank into her features as the color drained from them. "No," she said in a barely audible whisper, "I'm fine."

Father Russell began quickly to say the words of the sacrament, and she stood by him, gazing down at the dead man.

"I—I don't know where he is," she said. "He just put his head down." Her hands trembled over the cloth of her husband's shirt, which was open wide at the chest, and it was a moment before Father Russell understood that she was trying to button the shirt. But her hands were shaking too much. She patted the shirt down, then bowed her head and sobbed. Somewhere in the jangled apparatus of the room something was beeping, and he heard air rushing through pipes; everything was obscured in the intricacies of procedure. And then he was simply staring at the dead man's blank countenance, all sound and confusion and movement falling away from him. It was as though he had never looked at anything like this before; he remained quite still, in a profound quiet, for some minutes before Mrs. Simpson got his attention again. She had taken him by the wrist.

"Father," she was saying. "Father, he was a good man. God has taken him home, hasn't He?"

Father Russell turned to face the woman, to take her hands into his own and to whisper the words of hope.

"I THINK SEEING YOU there—at the hospital," he said to Tarmigian. "It upset me in an odd way."

"I cut my hand opening the paint jar," Tarmigian said. He was standing on a stepladder in the upstairs hallway of his rectory, painting the crown molding. Father Russell had walked out of his church in the chill of first frost and made his way across the little stone bridge and up the incline to the old man's door, had knocked and been told to enter, and, entering, finding no one, had reached back and knocked again.

"Up here," came Tarmigian's voice.

And the priest had climbed the stairs in a kind of torpor, his heart beating in his neck and face. He had blurted out that he wasn't feeling right, hadn't slept at all well, and finally he'd begun to hint at what he could divine as to why. He was now sitting on the top step, hat in hand, still carrying with him the sense of the long night he had spent, lying awake in the dark, seeing not the dead face of poor Mrs. Simpson's husband but Tarmigian holding up the bandaged hand and smiling. The image had wakened him each time he had drifted toward sleep.

"Something's happening to me," he said now, unable to believe himself.

The other man reached high with the paintbrush, concentrating. The ladder was rickety.

"Do you want me to hold the ladder?"

"Pardon me?"

"Nothing."

"Did you want to know if I wanted you to hold the ladder?"

"Well, do you?"

"You're worried I'll fall."

"I'd like to help."

"And did you say something is happening to you?"

Father Russell was silent.

"Forget the ladder, son."

"I don't understand myself lately," said the priest.

"Are you making me your confessor or something there, Reverend?"

"I—I can't—"

"Because I don't think I'm equipped."

"I've looked at the dead before," said Father Russell. "I've held the dying in my arms. I've never been very much afraid of it. I mean I've never been morbid."

"Morbidity is an indulgence."

"Yes, I know."

"Simply refuse to indulge yourself."

"I'm forty-three—"

"A difficult age, of course. You don't know whether you fit with the grown-ups or the children." Tarmigian paused to cough. He held the top step of the ladder with both hands, and his shoulders shook. Everything tottered. Then he stopped, breathed, wiped his mouth with the back of one hand.

Father Russell said, "I meant to say, I don't think I'm worried about myself."

"Well, that's good."

"I'm going to call and make you an appointment with a doctor."

"I'm fine. I've got a cold. I've coughed like this all my life."

"Nevertheless."

Tarmigian smiled at him. "You're a good man—but you're learning a tendency."

NO PEACE.

Father Russell had entered the priesthood without the sort of fervent sense of vocation he believed others had. In fact, he'd entertained serious doubts about it right up to the last year of seminary—doubts that, in spite of his confessor's reassurances to the contrary, he felt were more than the normal upsets of seminary life. In the first place, he had come to it against the wishes of his father, who had entertained dreams of a career in law for him; and while his mother applauded the decision, her own dream of grandchildren was visibly languishing in her eyes as the time for his final vows approached. Both parents had died within a month of each other during his last year of studies, and so there had been times when he'd had to contend with the added problem of an apprehension that he might unconsciously be learning to use his vocation as a form of refuge. But finally, nearing the end of his training, seeing the completion of the journey, something in him rejoiced, and he came to believe that this was what having a true vocation was: no extremes of emotion, no real perception of a break with the world, though the terms of his faith and the ancient ceremony that his training had prepared him to celebrate spoke of just that. He was even-tempered and confident, and when he was ordained, he set about the business of being a parish priest. There were matters to involve himself in, and he found that he could be energetic and enthusiastic about most of them. The life was satisfying in ways he hadn't expected, and if in his less confident moments some part of him entertained the suspicion that he was not progressing spiritually, he was also not the sort of man to go very deeply into such questions: there were things to do. He was not a contemplative. Or he hadn't been.

Something was shifting in his soul.

Nights were terrible. He couldn't even pray now. He stood at his rectory window and looked at the light in the old man's window, and his imagination presented him with the belief that he could hear the faint rattle of the deep cough, though he knew it was impossible across that distance. When he said the morning mass, he leaned down over the host and had to work to remember the words. The stolid, calm faces of his parishioners were almost ugly in their absurd confidence in him, their smiles of happy expectation and welcome. He took their hospitality and their care of him as his due, and felt waves of despair at the ease of it, the habitual taste and lure of it, while all the time his body was aching in ways that filled him with dread and reminded him of Tarmigian's ravaged features.

Sunday morning early, it began to rain. Someone called, then hung up before he could answer. He had been asleep; the loud ring at that hour had frightened him, changed his heartbeat. He took his own pulse, then stood at his window and gazed at the darkened shape of Tarmigian's church. That morning after the second mass, exhausted, miserable, filled with apprehension, he crossed the bridge in the rain, made his way up the hill and knocked on the old man's door. There wasn't any answer. He peered through the window on the porch and saw that there were dishes on the table in the kitchen, which was visible through the arched hallway off the living room. Tarmigian's Bible lay open on the arm of the easy chair. Father Russell knocked loudly and then walked around the building, into the church itself. It was quiet. The wind stirred outside and sounded like traffic whooshing by. Father Russell could feel his own heartbeat in the pit of his stomach. He sat down in the last pew of Tarmigian's church and tried to calm himself. Perhaps ten minutes went by, and then he heard voices. The old man was coming up the walk outside, talking to someone. Father Russell stood, thought absurdly of trying to hide, but then the door was opened and Tarmigian walked in, accompanied by an old woman in a white woolen shawl. Tarmigian had a big umbrella, which he shook down and folded, breathing heavily from the walk and looking, as always, even in the pall of his decline, amused by something. He hadn't seen Father Russell yet, though the old woman had. She nodded and smiled broadly, her hands folded neatly over a small black purse.

"Well," Tarmigian said. "To what do we owe this honor, Reverend?"

It struck Father Russell that they might be laughing at him. He dismissed this thought and, clearing his throat, said, "I—I wanted to see you." His own voice sounded stiffly formal and somehow foolish to him. He cleared his throat again.

"This is Father Russell," Tarmigian said loudly to the old woman. Then he touched her shoulder and looked at the priest. "Mrs. Aldenberry."

"God bless you," Mrs. Aldenberry said.

"Mrs. Aldenberry wants a divorce," Tarmigian murmured.

"Eh?" she said. Then, turning to Father Russell, "I'm hard of hearing."

"She wants her own television set," Tarmigian whispered.

"Pardon me?"

"And her own room."

"I'm hard of hearing," she said cheerfully to the priest. "I'm deaf as a post."

"Irritates her husband," Tarmigian said.

"I'm sorry," said the woman, "I can't hear a thing."

Tarmigian guided her to the last row of seats, and she sat down there, folded her hands in her lap. She seemed quite content, quite trustful, and the old minister, beginning to stutter into a deep cough, winked at Father Russell—as if to say this was all very entertaining. "Now," he said, taking the priest by the elbow, "let's get to the flattering part of all this—you walking over here getting yourself all wet because you're worried about me."

"I just wanted to stop by," Father Russell said. He was almost pleading. The old man's face, in the dim light, looked appallingly bony and pale.

"Look at you," said Tarmigian. "You're shaking."

Father Russell could not speak.

"Are you all right?"

The priest was assailed by the feeling that the older man found him somehow ridiculous—and he remembered the initial sense he'd had, when Tarmigian and Mrs. Aldenberry had entered, that he was being laughed at. "I just wanted to see how you were doing," he said.

"I'm a little under the weather," Tarmigian said, smiling.

And it dawned on Father Russell, with the force of a physical blow, that the old man knew quite well he was dying.

Tarmigian indicated Mrs. Aldenberry with a nod of his head. "Now I have to attend to the depths of this lady's sorrow. You know, she says she should've listened to her mother and not married Mr. Aldenberry fifty-two years ago. She's revising her own history; she can't remember being happy in all that time, not now, not after what's happened. Now you think about that a bit. Imagine her standing in a room slapping her forehead and saying 'What a mistake!' Fifty-two years. Oops. A mistake. She's glad she woke up in time. Think of it! And I'll tell you, Reverend, I think she feels lucky."

Mrs. Aldenberry made a prim, throat-clearing sound, then stirred in her seat, looking at them.

"Well," Tarmigian said, straightening, wiping the smile from his face. He offered his hand to the priest. "Shake hands. No. Let's embrace. Let's give this poor woman an ecumenical thrill."

Father Russell shook hands, then walked into the old man's extended arms. It felt like a kind of collapse. He was breathing the odor of bay rum and talcum and something else, too, something indefinable and dark, and to his astonishment he found himself fighting back tears. The two men stood there while Mrs. Aldenberry watched, and Father Russell was unable to control the sputtering and trembling that took hold of him. When Tarmigian broke the embrace, the priest turned away, trying to compose himself. Tarmigian was coughing again.

"Excuse me," said Mrs. Aldenberry. She seemed quite tentative and upset.

Tarmigian held up one hand, still coughing, and his eyes had grown wide with the effort to breathe.

"Hot honey with a touch of lemon and whiskey," she said, to no one in particular. "Works like a charm."

Father Russell thought about how someone her age would indeed learn to feel that humble folk remedies were effective in stopping illness. It was logical and reasonable, and he was surprised by the force of his own resentment of her for it. He stood there wiping his eyes and felt his heart constrict with bitterness.

"Well," Tarmigian said, getting his breath back.

"Hot toddy," said Mrs. Aldenberry. "Never knew it to fail." She was looking from one to the other of the two men, her expression taking on something of the look of tolerance. "Fix you up like new," she said, turning her attention to the priest, who could not stop blubbering. "What's—what's going on here?"

Father Russell had a moment of sensing that everything Tarmigian had done or said over the past year was somehow freighted with this one moment, and it took him a few seconds to recognize the implausibility of such a thing: no one could have planned it, or anticipated it, this one seemingly aimless gesture of humor—out of a habit of humorous gestures, and from a brave old man sick to death—that could feel so much like health, like the breath of new life.

He couldn't stop crying. He brought out a handkerchief and covered his face with it, then wiped his forehead. It had grown quiet. The other two were gazing at him. He straightened, caught his breath. "Excuse me."

"No excuse needed," Tarmigian said, looking down. His smile seemed vaguely uncertain now, and sad. Even a little afraid.

"What is going on here?" the old woman wanted to know.

"Why, nothing at all out of the ordinary," Tarmigian said, shifting the small weight of his skeletal body, clearing his throat, managing to speak very loudly, very gently, so as to reassure her, but making certain, too, that she could hear him.

Hannah Green

from

Golden Spark, Little Saint

SHE IS THE sacred center. Around her the wheel of the story with its thousand starry spokes spins. It might begin at any time, from the hour that she was born at Agen in December of the year 290 to the hour of her young martyr-death less than thirteen years later, or since, at as many shining points as there are gemstones on the reliquary statue, which holds her head, or silver nails in arabesques on the coffer that holds her body's bones; but the story opens now in the mountains of the Rouergue here at Conques, where, since before the turn of the Millennium, her bones have been enshrined and guarded.

For here we came first as travelers, Jack and I, in the springtime of 1975, to have our hearts caught unawares and to return—Jack a painter, a Californian by birth; I a writer, an Ohioan from an old Swedenborgian and Episcopalian background, a stranger to saints; and yet I was given through Sainte Foy, here in this remote and ancient place of pilgrimage, the gift of seeing into that zone which has been held sacred since the beginning of human consciousness.

WHEN WE FIRST came here, we came from the south, from Provence, where we had been staying that winter in a house in the olive groves of the wild white-stone Alpilles. It was our first year abroad together and we had fallen in love with Provence, with the country around us as far as Les Baux and Glanum and St.-Rémy and Avignon, as far as Arles and the Camargue and Les-Saintes-Maries-de-la-Mer at the edge of the sea. It was a kind of rapturous pagan love that extended outward to become a delight in all of France and the desire to see (and learn) all we could.

Yet an image of Sainte Foy gleaned almost by chance from a conversation among friends standing on the red Kirghiz in front of our fire one winter evening there on the Route du Destet had caught hold of my imagination, and I felt we must come here to Conques in particular to see her. There was something in my image of her that was deeper, older, more secret to me, more central, and that set her apart from the joyous openness of my love for Provence and its mystique. It was as if I felt her to be like a beloved sacred doll I had lost a long time ago. I had not seen a photograph of her, but somehow—stiff and gold and encrusted with jewels—she burned like a garnet with her own light in the night of my mind.

I read what little I found about her in our green Michelin *Guide to the Auvergne*, and in Muirhead's *Blue Guide to the South of France* (1926), given to us in New York by older writer friends who had lived in France in the twenties (among the surrealists), as we in the seventies sailed off on our fellowship year; but even had I learned more in advance, I still would not have been prepared.

Coming here we had crossed the Cevennes and stopped at Albi for two nights, and the smooth and sinuous red-brick fortress cathedral at

Albi was still strong in my mind when we arrived here late that April afternoon.

All afternoon as we drove northeast across the high rolling green plains from Albi to Rodez, it had been sunny, but here, twenty-five miles north of Rodez, where suddenly, after St.-Cyprien, we entered the dark stone gorges of the Dourdou and, after several miles, began to climb the steep ascent to Conques, here it had been raining shortly before we arrived. The street was wet. The slate-stone roofs glistened with water. The air felt clean like mountain air, and when we opened the casement windows of our room in the Hôtel Sainte Foy and looked out onto the steep roof across the narrow street, and up to the yellow stone church looming silent above it, I thought we had arrived in heaven.

I was in a trance of joy as we rushed out to see the statue of Sainte Foy before closing time. We bought our tickets and hurried across the cloister, barely pausing.

Then we entered the Treasure and there, in that room, which she makes holy and mysterious, there she was, at the end of the room through the high arch on her dais. There she was, all alone like a fragile child reaching out, entranced.

In that stilled moment, awed and torn with tenderness, the top gone from my head, I saw not only her, Sainte Foy, but shadowy figures around her. They were standing, tall and slightly bowed, dark presences without substance, like guardian angels, not clearly defined, but there, even as the monks who watched over her through the ages, even as the Ancient of Days.

I could feel the stirrings of that long procession of human beings who had come here down through time to fall on their knees and pray for her help, again and again in their devotion renewing her life—this eternal girl child, daughter becoming woman, who held within the promise of all that is good and beautiful and healing, and all that is bountiful.

FOR A LONG while I did not think that I could speak of this, not even to Jack. And even after I began to write this, my Book of Sainte Foy, I thought for a time that what I had seen then was too sacred, too tremulously personal, to be written down and woven into the work. I did not then know from whom it came, my vision, entering my mind's heart in a wave full with light, and engendering all that would grow from it—at first through reading, and then through our returns, our long sojourns here.

Now, crossing the cloister, I watch a breeze flowing upward through the leafy green woods of the gorge wall beyond the Ouche. The chestnuts are coming into bloom and soon the woods will be burgeoning with the pale yellow sprays of their lovely Roman-candle blossoms. The dog starts to bark again down at the trout farm at the bottom of the gorge.

When I enter the Treasure, Père André in his white monk's robe is sitting in the chair in his little library which adjoins the entrance. An ample solid man of more than sixty years, gentle and balding, he has fallen asleep for a moment after lunch. I pray for his health as I pass, and for his long life. He has been very kind.

No one is in the room as I enter, no one save Sainte Foy that is, and I walk directly up to the raised altar-like place through the high arch, where she sits holding out her delicate gold hands which hold tiny tube vases for flowers, her arms outstretched from the elbow, shyly, as if to receive one, yet a little tentatively. One must come close, but one may come no closer than the invisible flowers.

Today one of the lights that illumines her has gone out, and she has never looked lovelier. Shadows become her—little virgin, very pure, who died for her faith when she was but twelve. So they sang of her in sacred canticles, for so she answered the Proconsul Dacian, although she knew she would die for it: "My name," she said, "is Faith. And I am a Christian." That was at Agen in the year 303, in the reign of the Emperor Diocletian, at the time of the last of the terrible persecutions—the Great Persecution, it was called.

And she is here now, for her bones worked miracles. She was brought here to Conques, to this remote abbey in the mountains of the Rouergue, from Agen on the Garonne, where the coastal plains begin, more than one hundred miles to the west of here. She was brought here sometime between the years 864 and 882 by the monk Aronisde, called since that time the Pious Robber and the Author of the Furtive Translation.

It was her holy bones he stole, together with other remains—her belt, a little purse, a few amber beads, and bits of woven cloth, the precious tissues the Christians had used to wipe the blood from her skin when, in the night of her death, secretly, they took her decapitated body from the public square to a hidden place away from the city, high on the rock plateau called Pompejac.

"There they could not bury her body," they would sing in the Song of Sainte Foy written down in the Provençal (or the ancient Occitan as they prefer to say now in this country) of the eleventh century. "They made a kind of nest for it like that which the ostrich makes in summer, and entombed her thus in the rocks. They wept, grieving with their tears so piously, watering the ground around her humble sepulcher. They had no means to honor her better. Sorrowful they were, and miserable, grieving. They were anguished, like fugitives, guarding her tomb by day and by night, afraid the evil would come again."

And she is here now, the bones of her head within the heart of her statue. She is here now, looking out of her smooth gold face with her dark obsidian slightly slanted eyes, looking out from across the centuries with an expression of majestic courage, with the expression of one whose mind is on eternity, while yet she hears the beating of our hearts.

She is here, protected by glass on her dais, and still somehow the Energy of Life flows into her through her raised and partly open hands, through her thumbs and forefingers and the tiny tube vases, the unseen flowers, and outward toward whomsoever may come to her.

Touching, stiff, tiny figure less than three feet in height, her head is large, her body small, thin; not a likeness in any ordinary sense, her statue is, rather, symbolic. It is a shrine. And in some mystic way it suggests to the mind's eye more strongly than any imagined likeness could the presence of Sainte Foy herself as she was, with her young skin freshness and the radiance, the life in her face, the light, and as she is: bone and spirit come to God.

Here she sits like a sacred child bravely bearing the rich and fragile finery made to adorn her, like a queen, sovereign yet delicate, tender and gentle, but with a wild, mysterious power. Bride of Christ, she holds the Mystery of the Word within her—*La Majesté de Sainte Foy, Maiestas Sanctae Fidis*, seated on her throne and bearing on her person in gold and precious stones, in carved intaglios and cameos, the splendor and magic of the ages, come to her from ancient times, and places far off—to the East and the South—from Rome, from Egypt, from Greece and the Holy Land, from Persia, Byzantium, the Spain of the Moors, and from the griffin-guarded land of the Scythians, treasures of Kings and Emperors of Old, treasures brought home to France by the Crusaders, treasures of Barbarian Warriors, and of the ancient Gallo-Romans, those poets and masters of eloquence, who once traveled the whole civilized world and returned home to their great estates with their vineyards and their fine libraries, which then in the fifth and sixth centuries were ravaged, burned, taken over entirely by the invaders from the north, treasures plundered, bought, traded, guarded in castles and holy places, bestowed, received, treasures carried off secretly by the fleeing Gaulish refugees and handed down then from generation to generation from antiquity down through the Dark Ages, until they came to rest on her, brought by pilgrims from far and near who came here in their need and with their fears to adore her in fervor and seek her protection, for her healings and her blessings knew no bounds.

Oh, radiant saint! Still after centuries the bones of her mind, the stuff of her soul breathe her life, her presence into this, her reliquary statue, which is the work of many hands over many a hundred years, all drawn and inspired by this little holy martyr: Sainte Foy.

"Generatrice of art," Père André calls her. The exact date of the consecration of her statue is lost; the origin of her head is shrouded in mystery, but her statue was here already in the year 940, when, it is recorded in the abbey's cartulary, Étienne II, Abbot of Conques, son of Robert, Viscount of the Auvergne, having been elected Bishop of Clermont-Ferrand, and soon to complete the cathedral he was building there, prepared to effect the solemn translation of her mortal remains. But she would not be moved. She was heavy as a mountain, and as firmly implanted.

Three times they gathered in as many weeks, the monks of the abbey, the bishops and notable lords of the Rouergue and all the Auvergne, three times they gathered, having fasted and cleansed themselves of all sins and possible sinners, three times they gathered before the altar of the Holy Saviour, and although each time their prayers were more fervent, and the chanting of the litanies and the psalms was more heavenly and prolonged, still when they attempted to remove her, neither she nor her holy casket could be budged, not even an inch. The bells of the church rang out and angels sang somewhere aloft as it was concluded by the learned churchmen that it was her wish to remain where she was at Conques and God's will that she do so.

All wonderfully wrought and filigreed and inlaid with jewels and precious enamels, the work went on for more than seven hundred years. The latest scholarly investigation—that undertaken by Jean Taralon, Director General of the Bureau of Historic Monuments, at the time of her restoration in 1954 – determined that her body of wood had received its first covering of gold before the ninth century was out. Her arms and hands and the tiny tube vases were fashioned in the sixteenth century, replacing earlier arms and hands with bracelets. But her head is older. It is thought to date from the fourth century, the century of her martyrdom, and is made of gold repoussé laid over with gold leaf. Although the fashioning of the hair makes the work appear to be Byzantine, and her head is thought to have been originally that of a late

Roman god-emperor, laurel-crowned, her face is the mask of a Celtic god or goddess; and through this head originally not her own, through its dark enamel eyes, blue as midnight, her spirit emanates with mysterious, radiant calm.

"Generatrice of art," Père André calls her. And he speaks of her "luminous life of prayer."

Somehow her genius breathed through the hands of that first worker who began to give her shape, so that as he formed her little body from two pieces of wood of the root of the yew tree he joined at mid-thigh, working with his chisel, smoothing over with his rasp, hollowing out the cavity in her back to enclose the bones of her mind, he caught the very presence of her spirit, so that although he was not skilled at carving statues, but rather (it is thought) had worked his life long making wooden shoes and other useful objects, still by the very accidents of his innocence and with his innate awe and love, in the rush to form her he had defined her shape to receive the golden clothing in such a way that he'd caught her very breath and her particular power; and when the god-head he'd held and measured at the neck, when it was fitted on over the wooden neck he'd shaped and smoothed for it, her head (which, centuries later, critics would note was too large for her body) was tilted in such a way (thought also to be awkward) that it would convey the sense of her listening with Christ encompassed in her rapt mind, the very skull of which, bound with strips of silver and wrapped in imperial purple silk brocaded in Byzantium, was ritually enclosed within her statue.

By the presence of her relic, then, she was mystically there to imbue the antique head of her statue with her own grace and trance-like power, which could be, was, and even now sometimes is thaumaturgic.

"Generatrice of art," Père André says. She was here as magnet, here as source. To her came the crown of Charles the Child to become the crown of her martyrdom, and the golden doves of the Abbot of Beaulieu to adorn her throne. To her came the builders, the sculptors, the poets. To her came the goldsmiths who worked through the years embroidering her golden gown and outlining her full falling sleeves, her collar, her hem with pearls of gold, and setting the whole with gemstones of every color until, encrusted, she shone with a light like that of the heavenly Jerusalem—with emeralds, marvelously luminous; with rubies and garnets which, the ancients believed, shone with their own light; with sapphires, pearls, topazes, opals, and hyacinths blue as the sky; with jade and Byzantine bloodstones; with beryl green as sea foam; with jasper of magical properties, and nicolo; with carnelians, and amethysts, ribboned agates, and cloisonné enamels; with onyx and sardonyx, which with its three colors, red, white, and black, signified, according to the eleventh-century poet Marbodus, those who carried in their minds the memory of Christ's passion. To her came crystals clear as water, and crystal balls like that found with the grave goods of Childeric, the last of the pagan Merovingian kings (died 482). To her came he who thought to set the aquamarine in the shape of a tear in the center of her forehead in the gold-beaded net that binds her hair—the tear she shed at the last moment, this young girl who so loved life she went, fired in her love, insisting on the truth, into her passion and eternity.

Brought before the Proconsul Dacian at Agen on the sixth of October in the year 303, she said, "My name is Faith, and I am a Christian."

She said, "Since I was a little child and first learned of Him, I have loved the Lord Jesus Christ."

She said, "I have served Him in every way as best I could."

And Dacian, for the girl they had led to stand trial before him was so young, of noble blood, and the most perfect beauty—luminous as a white flower and radiant with roses in her cheeks—Dacian said, "Your mother and father await you now in the house of your birth. Think of the grief you would cause them. You their beloved daughter, their first-born."

"It is Him my soul loveth," she said. "His name is Adonai."

"Fides, your earthly time passed as swiftly as that of a flower that lives but a day," opens a canticle of old sung by the Christians in her great church.

"Come, come, my child," said Dacian, "sacrifice to Diana as your parents would have you do."

"I pray you, Lord, help me now as you promised," she said, and with her three fingers she made the sign of the cross.

"No," she said in a voice of great strength, "no, I will not."

Then Dacian spoke seductively. Quietly, almost whispering, he said, "Ere long your parents shall prepare for you the wedding gown and ointments. The bridegroom will await you, and in the nuptial chamber the lamps will burn for you. The perfume of love shall be there, the branches of hawthorn, and love you shall breathe as your bridegroom embraces you. The beloved task of bearing children shall be yours, and you shall be blessed."

And Fides, her voice clear and natural, replied, "I want to take pleasure in my Lord, it is with Him I want to laugh and be gay, it is Him I would take as bridegroom, whether it pleases you or not; for to me He is fair, to me He is altogether lovely. I will not lie: if I cannot have Him there is nothing that will heal me." (So have her words, recalling the imagery of the Song of Songs, come down to us in the Song of Sainte Foy.)

"Come now, my child," said Dacian, "you speak so charmingly. I have no wish to torture a girl as tender as you. Come sacrifice to the goddess, sacrifice to Diana. You need only reach out your fingers and touch a grain of the salt and the incense placed on the altar there before you. Do that. Just that. And I shall release you."

A hush fell over the mob. Fides did not move her hand.

"Thus would the State have it!" said Dacian.

Holding her young head high there amid the symbols of power, Fides spoke to the Tribunal; and not only Dacian but the whole great crowd assembled in the square at Agen that day heard her. "Your gods and goddesses are but daemons," she said. "They are evil spirits. As their statues are the work of men's hands, they are the product of men's imaginings.

Neither are your emperors gods: Diocletian as Jupiter, and Maximian, his Hercules, are only men, and corrupt men at that. As are you, cruel Lord Dacian.

"There is but one God—He who came down from heaven for us and made Himself man very gifted, who healed the sick and the leprous and gave us baptism in water, He who suffered and died for us on the cross, and rose again from the dead, destroying dark hell, and went unto the Father.

"No, I will not sacrifice to Diana, nor will I touch your incense."

And as the torture was prepared, and again later walking toward the block, her white throat held high—the exquisite skin—she spoke as she would in her Song, saying, "It is Him I would take as Bridegroom . . . for to me He is fair, to me He is altogether lovely."

Sainte Foy, virgin and martyr, pray for us.
Sainte Foy, beloved of God, pray for us.

Prayers whispered across the ages. Prayers whispered in their time in a thousand chapels dedicated to Sainte Foy across the face of Europe and along the great pilgrim route to Saint Jacques (Santiago) de Compostelle. Prayers chanted in Latin and sung as hymns, prayers shouted, cried out, sobbed forth in the language of the people here, in the Languedoc, prayers borne here silently by those who came with their precious stones to pin them, as it were, like flowers with their burning hopes onto her golden gown.

Alice Walker

FAITH

The Welcome Table

FOR SISTER CLARA WARD

I'm going to sit at the Welcome table
Shout my troubles over
Walk and talk with Jesus
Tell God how you treat me
One of these days!

Spiritual

THE OLD WOMAN stood with eyes uplifted in her Sunday-go-to-meeting clothes: high shoes polished about the tops and toes, a long rusty dress adorned with an old corsage, long withered, and the remnants of an elegant silk scarf as headrag stained with grease from the many oily pigtails underneath. Perhaps she had known suffering. There was a dazed and sleepy look in her aged blue-brown eyes. But for those who searched hastily for "reasons" in that old tight face, shut now like an ancient door, there was nothing to be read. And so they gazed nakedly upon their own fear transferred; a fear of the black and the old, a terror of the unknown as well as of the deeply known. Some of those who saw her there on the church steps spoke words about her that were hardly fit to be heard, others held their pious peace; and some felt vague stirrings of pity, small and persistent and hazy, as if she were an old collie turned out to die.

She was angular and lean and the color of poor gray Georgia earth, beaten by king cotton and the extreme weather. Her elbows were wrinkled and thick, the skin ashen but durable, like the bark of old pines. On her face centuries were folded into the circles around one eye, while around the other, etched and mapped as if for print, ages more threatened again to live. Some of them there at the church saw the age, the dotage, the missing buttons down the front of her mildewed black dress. Others saw cooks, chauffeurs, maids, mistresses, children denied or smothered, in the deferential way she held her cheek to the side, toward the ground. Many of them saw jungle orgies in an evil place, while others were reminded of riotous anarchists looting and raping in the streets. Those who knew the hesitant creeping up on them of the law, saw the beginning of the end of the sanctuary of Christian worship, saw the desecration of Holy Church, and saw an invasion of privacy, which they struggled to believe they still kept.

Still she had come down the road toward the big white church alone. Just herself, an old forgetful woman, nearly blind with age. Just her and her eyes raised dully to the glittering cross that crowned the sheer silver steeple. She had walked along the road in a stagger from her house a half-mile away. Perspiration, cold and clammy, stood on her brow and along the creases by her thin wasted nose. She stopped to calm herself on the wide front steps, not looking about her as they might have expected her to do, but simply standing quite still, except for a slight quivering of her throat and tremors that shook her cotton-stockinged legs.

The reverend of the church stopped her pleasantly as she stepped into the vestibule. Did he say, as they thought he did, kindly, "Auntie, you know this is not your church?" As if one could choose the wrong one. But no one remembers, for they never spoke of it afterward, and she brushed past him anyway, as if she had been brushing past him all her life, except this time she was in a hurry. Inside the church she sat on the very first bench from the back, gazing with concentration at the stained-glass window over her head. It was cold, even inside the church, and she was shivering. Everybody could see. They stared at her as they came in and sat down near the front. It was cold, very cold to them, too; outside the church it was below freezing and not much above inside. But the sight of her, sitting there somehow passionately ignoring them, brought them up short, burning.

The young usher, never having turned anyone out of his church before, but not even considering this job as *that* (after all, she had no right to be there, certainly), went up to her and whispered that she should leave. Did he call her "Grandma," as later he seemed to recall he had? But for those who actually hear such traditional pleasantries and to whom they actually mean something, "Grandma" was not one, for she did not pay him any attention, just muttered, "Go 'way," in a weak sharp *bothered* voice, waving his frozen blond hair and eyes from near her face.

It was the ladies who finally did what to them had to be done. Daring their burly decisive husbands to throw the old colored woman out, they made their point. God, mother, country, earth, church. It involved all that, and well they knew it. Leather-bagged and -shoed, with good calf-skin gloves to keep out the cold, they looked with contempt at the bloodless gray arthritic hands of the old woman, clenched loosely, restlessly in her lap. Could their husbands expect them to sit up in church with *that*? No, no, the husbands were quick to answer and even quicker to do their duty.

Under the old woman's arms they placed their hard fists (which afterward smelled of decay and musk—the fermenting scent of onion skins and rotting greens). Under the old woman's arms they raised their fists, flexed their muscular shoulders, and out she flew through the door, back under the cold blue sky. This done, the wives folded their healthy arms across their trim middles and felt at once justified and scornful. But none of them said so, for none of them ever spoke of the incident again. Inside the church it was warmer. They sang, they prayed. The protection and promise of God's impartial love grew more, not less, desirable as the sermon gathered fury and lashed itself out above their penitent heads.

THE OLD WOMAN stood at the top of the steps looking about in bewilderment. She had been singing in her head. They had interrupted her. Promptly she began to sing again, though this time a sad song. Suddenly, however, she looked down the long gray highway and saw something interesting and delightful coming. She started to grin, toothlessly, with short giggles of joy, jumping about and slapping her hands on her knees. And soon it became apparent why she was so happy. For coming down the highway at a firm though leisurely pace was Jesus. He was wearing an immaculate white long dress trimmed in gold around the neck and hem, and a red, a bright red, cape. Over his left arm he carried a brilliant blue blanket. He was wearing sandals and a beard and he had long brown hair parted on the right side. His eyes, brown, had wrinkles around them as if he smiled or looked at the sun a lot. She would have known him, recognized him, anywhere. There was a sad but joyful look to his face, like a candle was glowing behind it, and he walked with sure even steps in her direction, as if he were walking on the sea. Except that he was not carrying in his arms a baby sheep, he looked exactly like that picture of him that she had hanging over her bed at home. She had taken it out of a white lady's Bible while she was working for her. She had looked at that picture for more years than she could remember, but never once had she really expected to see him. She squinted her eyes to be sure he wasn't carrying a little sheep in one arm, but he was not. Ecstatically she began to wave her arms for fear he would miss seeing her, for he walked looking straight ahead on the shoulder of the highway, and from time to time looking upward at the sky.

All he said when he got up close to her was, "Follow me," and she bounded down to his side with all the bob and speed of one so old. For every one of his long determined steps she made two quick ones. They walked along in deep silence for a long time. Finally she started telling him about how many years she had cooked for them, cleaned for them, nursed them. He looked at her kindly but in silence. She told him indignantly about how they had grabbed her when she was singing in her head and not looking, and how they had tossed her out of his church. A old heifer like me, she said, straightening up next to Jesus, breathing hard. But he smiled down at her and she felt better instantly and time just seemed to fly by. When they passed her house, forlorn and sagging, weatherbeaten and patched, by the side of the road, she did not even notice it, she was so happy to be out walking along the highway with Jesus.

She broke the silence once more to tell Jesus how glad she was that he had come, how she had often looked at his picture hanging on her wall (she hoped he didn't know she had stolen it) over her bed, and how she had never expected to see him down here in person. Jesus gave her one of his beautiful smiles and they walked on. She did not know where they were going; someplace wonderful, she suspected. The ground was like clouds under their feet, and she felt she could walk forever without becoming the least bit tired. She even began to sing out loud some of the old spirituals she loved, but she didn't want to annoy Jesus, who looked so thoughtful, so she quieted down. They walked on, looking straight over the treetops into the sky, and the smiles that played over her dry wind-cracked face were like first clean ripples across a stagnant pond. On they walked without stopping.

THE PEOPLE IN church never knew what happened to the old woman; they never mentioned her to one another or to anybody else. Most of them heard sometime later that an old colored woman fell dead along the highway. Silly as it seemed, it appeared she had walked herself to death. Many of the black families along the road said they had seen the old lady high-stepping down the highway; sometimes jabbering in a low insistent voice, sometimes singing, sometimes merely gesturing excitedly with her hands. Other times silent and smiling, looking at the sky. She had been alone, they said. Some of them wondered aloud where the old woman had been going so stoutly that it had worn her heart out. They guessed maybe she had relatives across the river, some miles away, but none of them really knew.

Ron Hansen

from

Mariette in Ecstasy

Mass of the Apparition of Our Lady of Lourdes

Whispers of pellet snow on the ice.

Late morning. A half-rim of moon is faint in a mica-blue sky.

Winter shag blows as a Morgan horse roughs his hoary jaw against a water trough and grandly suffers the zero cold.

A gray-and-white cat cautiously steps down from a roof peak and settles against a chimney stack, its paws turned primly underneath its breast.

Sister Geneviève is in a poor-box overcoat as she totters up from a shack with both hands on a heavy tin pail of coal.

Sisters Monique, Virginie, and Antoinette are sipping hot barley tea in the infirmary after an hour in the weather trying to repair the screw on a hundred-year-old winepress.

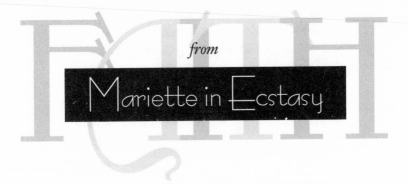

Window glass over the priest's sink is hatched and helixed with frost but sunshine is bristling on the shellacked windowsill and on a tarnished spoon, a green tin matchbox, and a stoppered chemist's phial holding brown flakes of dried blood. Eighth-inch lettering on the glass tube reads "American Pharmaceutical."

Ever so slowly the flakes ooze and redden until the phial holds blood again.

Mariette walks a toweled broom along a hallway by Sister Virginie's cell and then kneels below a horrid crucifixion that she hates, Christ's flesh-painted head like a block of woe, his black hair sleek as enamel and his black beard like ironweed, his round eyes bleary with pity and failure, and his frail form softly breasted and feminine and redly willowed in blood. And yet she prays, as she always does, *We adore you, O Christ, and we praise you, because by your holy cross you have redeemed the world.* And just then, she'll later tell Père Marriott, she is veiled in Christ's blessing and tenderness, she feels it flow down from her head like holy oil and thrill her skin like terror. Everything she has ever wished for seems to have been, in a hidden way, this. Entire years of her life are instantly there as if she could touch any hour of them, but she now sees Jesus present in her history as she hadn't before, kindness itself and everlastingly loyal, good father and friend and husband to her, hurting just as she hurt at times, pleased by her tiniest pleasures, wholly loving her common humanness and her essential uniqueness, so that the treacheries and sins and affronts of her past seem hideous to her and whatever good she's done seems as nothing compared to the shame she feels for her feckless-ness and indifference to him. And she is kneeling there in misery and sorrow when she opens her hands like a book and sees an intrusion of blood on both palms, pennies of skin turning redder and slowly rising up in blisters that in two or three minutes tear with the terrible pain of hammered nails, and then the hand flesh jerks with the fierce sudden weight of Christ's body and she feels the hot burn in both wrists. She feels her feet twisted behind her as both are transfixed with nails and the agony in both soles is as though she's stood in the rage of orange, glowing embers. She is breathless, she thirsts, she chills with loss of blood, and she hears Sister Dominique from a great distance, asking, "Are you ill?" when she feels an iron point rammed hard against her heart and she faints.

Hours later Mother Saint-Raphaël thinks it important that the most worshipful sisters see the postulant as she is and not as she is being imagined, so just after Vespers twelve of them slowly walk one by one through the infirmary and stare down at Mariette in infatuation and fear and relief as she stares up in a trance and seems to smile at their procession, and Sister Aimée permits them to softly touch Mariette's wrapped hands. Many ask if she is feeling much pain and Sister Aimée replies that the hurt must be excruciating. Each of them who asks for prayers is promised that she'll be remembered just as soon as Mariette wakes up.

And when all the sisters have walked through and Sister Aimée has been excused, Mother Saint-Raphaël installs a stool beside the headrail and with no more than a whisper of sound sits down beside Mariette and is as still as a picture for a while, as composed as a book of ritual, disarray's opposite, her handsome face neutral, her hard sandals flat on the floor, a hand gently inside a hand, intensely watching Mariette as the girl seems to hear harmonies inside her, as she seems to hover outside time. "Mariette?" Mother Saint-Raphaël finally asks. "Are you here now? Are you listening?"

She sees Mariette's dark lashes flutter a little, as if she's breathed over a candle flame. She pets a wisp of sable-brown hair away from the postulant's forehead and says, "It's Mother Saint-Raphaël. Your prioress."

Silver daggers of light shine in Mariette's blue irises and her mouth twitches slightly, as if she's heard and is trying to talk. The prioress is silent, then turns and twists hot water from a washrag and drags it frankly and affectionately over the postulant's too-white face, just as if she were suddenly blind and learning Mariette with her hands. Eventually Mariette opens her eyes.

"Was it the same this time?" the prioress asks.

Mariette thinks. "Yes."

"You were dwelling on Christ's passion."

She agrees.

Mother Saint-Raphaël bestows the washrag to a dish behind her and floats her manly, twisted hands atop her thighs. "Were you alone?"

"Yes."

"Was that necessary, do you think?"

Mariette looks at her carefully, in the half-wince of a pianist newly hearing the flaw in one key. "We find God in stillness and silence."

"I'm sorry," Mother Saint-Raphaël says. "I may have added a nuance I didn't intend."

Mariette hurtfully gets up to a sitting position and holds her wrapped hands just below her heart. She smiles understandingly as she says, "And yet you're suspicious still, aren't you."

"I have been troubled by God's motives for this," the prioress says. "I see no possible reasons for it. Is it so Mariette Baptiste will be praised and esteemed by the pious? Or is it so she shall be humiliated and jeered at by skeptics? Is it to honor religion or to humble science? And what are these horrible wounds, really? A trick of anatomy, a bleeding challenge to medical diagnosis, a brief and baffling injury that hasn't yet, in six hundred years, changed our theology or our religious practices. Have you any idea how disruptive you've been? You are awakening hollow talk and half-formed opinions that have no place in our priory, and I have no idea why God would be doing this to us. To you. I do know that the things the villagers have been giving us have not helped us in our vow of poverty. And all the seeking people who have been showing up have not helped our rule of enclosure. And there are breaches to our vow of obedience whenever you become the topic."

She sees that the postulant is staring at her impassively, with a hint, even, of amusement. She says in a sterner way, "I flatter myself that I have been extremely tolerant and patient, thus far. I have done so out of respect for your late sister, and in sympathy for the torment you have in her loss. But I shall not suffer your confusions much longer. And so I pray, Mariette, that if it is in your power to stop this—as I presume it is—that you do indeed stop it." She pauses and then stands. "And if it is in your power to heal me of the hate and envy I have for you now, please do that as well."

Mass of the Seven Holy Founders of the Servites, Confessors.

12 February 1907

Esteemed Reverend Marriott:
We the undersigned are of the firmest opinion that our blessed priory is being held hostage to a postulant's wiles and chicanery! We shall not have our convent contaminated by her! We shall not tolerate the favoritism and particular affection shown her thus far! We believe she possesses not one iota of orthodoxy and we beseech you, for the good of the younger souls here and for the future of our holy Church, to have her presented to a proper tribunal where, our prayers have assured us, her guile and stratagems will be found out. Although we harbor no ill feelings toward our saintly Mother Superior, we do have long memories and know that such as Mariette were quite readily dispatched by those glorious emissaries of God's will whose venerable portraits now grace the halls of our Motherhouse. We therefore beg of you to conquer the permissiveness and infirmity that is so rampant here and treat this hoax with the thoroughness and gravity it warrants.
Yours in humility,
Sr. Monique, Sr. Saint-Estèphe, Sr. Marthe, Sr. Honoré,
Sr. Marguerite, Sr. Saint-Stanislas, Sr. Félicité, Sr. Aimée

Ash Wednesday

Sister Zélie wanders down the hallway, drawling four fingers along the white wall, and then halting outside Mariette's cell, just as she knew she would. She hesitates and then goes inside and delights at being there, her callused hands softly touching down on the furniture as she might have rested them on the silken heads of infants. Everything is orderly, neat as a pin. She is pleased to smooth the gray blanket of the palliasse. She tips a water pitcher and is tempted to drink from it but does not. She holds a flutter in her stomach as she opens the armoire and presses her face to Mariette's habits, inhaling the delicious perfume that exudes from them. Sister Zélie is walking toward the secretary when a sandal catches on a finishing nail that shines from the flooring. She taps the nailhead with her heel and it drops; she kneels in order to pinch the nail, and lifts it without effort from its hole. And then she sees that the floor plank is freed and she furtively tips it up. She crushes her habit sleeve above her elbow and reaches down underneath the flooring to a joist. She pulls out a sheaf of handwritten pages tied up in a red satin ribbon.

She hears the floor creak and finds Mother Saint-Raphaël frowning into Mariette's cell from the hallway. Sister Zélie simpers and holds up the papers. "Look."

> I have been told to receive our hundreds of Sunday visitors in the parlor, but all who speak to me think I am insane. My head empties and I do not know how to reply to them. Surely Mother Superior must be demented to think me fit for such duties. I hold no conversations but those I have with you. I have no interest in people unless I see Jesus in them.
>
> Mother Saint-Raphaël has forbidden me Communion for six days now. Oh, how I ache for him, and how tortured and sick and desolate I have felt without him! I grieve to imagine how dull and haggard and ugly his Mariette must seem to him now! And yet I should think myself hateful if being deprived of him for these six days had not grossly disfigured me.
>
> What a cruel mistress I am to complain so much about your absence when I should be wooing you and praising you for your

kindnesses and sweet presence. You see, though, that I have become obsessed by you. You are not here with me enough if for one brief moment I have no sense of you. And yet I have only gratitude for the desperation you have caused me, and I loathe the peace in which I lived before I truly knew you.

—Well, there are hundreds more, as you know.

—Writing was a kind of prayer for me.

—Mother Saint-Raphaël was quite displeased. Another postulant may have been sent away.

—But I won't be?

—You have a cult.

At Matins, Sister Marguerite walks down from the choir with a red book and kneels before Mother Saint-Raphaël for a blessing before going to the green marble altar below Our Lady of Sorrows and reading: "'*The Constitution of the Second Order of the Sisters of the Crucifixion in Accordance with the Common Observance of the Rule of Saint Benedict.*

"'Chapter forty-six. Excommunication for faults.

"'If our sister is found to be at odds with the Holy Rule, or disobedient to her mother superior's directions, or otherwise detrimental to our way of perfection, she shall be admonished by her prioress in accordance with the Lord's injunction. Even then she may not redress her sins; if this be the case, she shall be reproved in public. If, however, there is still no transformation or amendment in her conduct, she shall be subject to excommunication.

"'She shall eat alone, when and how much in accordance with whatever the prioress deems proper. She shall not intone a psalm or antiphon or read a lesson in the oratory until she has been corrected. She shall work alone, dwelling with us in penance and sorrow. Eyes shall not communicate with her, she shall not be accompanied, she shall not be spoken to by hand or voice. She is not to be blessed as she passes, nor is her food to be blessed, nor is she to be blessed in common prayers except in pleas that God shall forgive her trespasses.

"'We hold out hope that these punishments may not bring her condemnation but health in mind and body. Ever mindful, however, of Saint Paul who said, "Put away the evil one from among you," and, "If the faithless one depart, let him depart," the prioress shall finally determine if our wayward sister shall be sent away permanently. We do these things so that one sheep may not infect our flock with her disease.'"

Mass of Saint Valentine, Priest and Martyr

Sister Aimée strolls behind Mariette as she walks achingly down the hallway in half-mittens and gray wool stockings, a hand holding her side. And then Mariette sees an hourglass and four stacked books just outside her cell, and Sister Zélie folding her black habits into a box. Sisters Sabine and Saint-Michel and Claudine are hauling out her pine armoire and the feet are chattering along the plank floor.

"Are they taking out everything?" Mariette asks.

Sister Claudine hesitantly stares and then continues with her tasks.

Sister Zélie is haphazardly putting white towels into the box while pretending she hasn't heard. Written in the prioress's hand and tacked up on the door is a paper scrap that reads: "She is to be delivered over for the destruction of the flesh, that her spirit may be saved in the day of the Lord. Saint Paul, 1 Corinthians 5:5."

Mariette turns to Sister Aimée, but she knowingly walks down the hallway to a four-by-six closet that held priests' vestments and thuribles and monstrances and homely paintings but is now completely empty save for a holy water stoup and a palliasse rolled up underneath a simple wooden cross.

"You'll be staying here," Sister Aimée says.

"Why?"

"Mother Superior orders it."

"Why here, I mean? Why not some other place?"

Sister Aimée frowns at Mariette's innocence and then she finds the interior door with one hand. Eight tall iron bars firmly clank against an iron lockplate and change the closet into a jail.

Sister Marthe tiredly walks down the hall in the flooding darkness of first rising and pauses to tap the castanets in her hand before whining, "In the name of God, my sisters, let us rise!" She hears four or five of them reciting, "His holy name be praised!" and she proceeds down the hallway as if she were dully reentering sleep. When she passes Mariette's jail cell, however, she cannot resist looking in. She is just there in the corner, undressed still and kneeling on the hard floor like the night terror in a child's closet, her wild brown hair all thrash and storm, her hands hidden behind her back, her stare as serious as torture. She smiles insincerely at Sister Marthe and says, "*Benedicite,*" and Sister Marthe hurriedly walks on.

—I have no memories of that.

—You deny it then?

—Each tale I hear is a place I haven't been.

Mass of the Flight into Egypt

Walking in procession, the sisters go into the tallow-lit refectory for collation, hesitating only to raise their habits slightly and step over Mariette whose penance it is to lie facedown on the dining hall floor, like the shoe-black door to a dark, dank cellar where fruit blooms in the jars.

And at the first rising she is prostrate on the great red Persian carpet as the sisters walk in pairs from the nave and genuflect just short of her and go up into the choirs for Matins and Lauds. Each one tries not to look, and yet each one sees her. She pulls their eyes like the print on a page. She is the stillness that ends their prayers. She is as present to them as God.

Mass of Saint Simeon, Bishop, Martyr

Walking nowhere in particular, Sisters Anne, Claudine, and Sabine talk solemnly about their own imperfections and slosh through fresh snow past the stiff, whitened cattails of the marsh and the white paws of the firs, and past the old printery sunk to its sills in snow and weed wrack and wind spew and ruin. And when they sit it's on a stone bench in the cemetery, in the company of forty-one names, including the first Sister Geneviève, a prioress, and another Sister Saint-Michel, born in Amiens, France. Sister Sabine is drawing houses with a stick when she gets the feeling they're being watched, and she turns to see that the postulant is just beside Mother Céline's fresh grave and starkly black against the white stage of the snow and the green curtain of pine woods, but glamorously alone and forlorn like a pretty girl about to sing, and with all the sisters listening.

"Don't look," Sister Sabine says, but they do, and Mariette lifts her hands as if she's written on the palms. Each turns away.

Mass of Saint Gabriel of Our Lady of Sorrows, Confessor

Mariette in ecstasy.

She's been seated on an ottoman in the chapter room in the Great Silence following Compline, and she's poised there while Sisters Philomène and Hermance recruit Sisters Geneviève and Léocadie to confirm their witness. Each approaches Mariette reverently and sits with perfect faith and attention, trying to share in the Christ she is seeing as she stares at a spot just above their heads.

"Where are you?" Sister Philomène whispers.

"Sitting in choir," she says, "with the Psalter."

"And is Jesus there?"

"Yes."

Sister Léocadie asks, "Oh, what does he look like?"

"Handsome," she says.

Sister Hermance hushes her voice while insisting, "You have to tell us what's happening!"

"Christ takes the book," Mariette says, "and sings the psalms in Hebrew, in the high tenor of the cantors, just as he did in his childhood."

She gets up. She walks over to a tallow candle. She pinches out the flame. She goes to another and extinguishes that one, too. Everywhere around her there is darkness. She tells them, "He holds my hand in his and we two walk down the hallway to his house inside ours. Which is his heart."

Sister Philomène turns and sees Mother Saint-Raphaël halted at the door. She worriedly prepares to stand and curtsy, but she sees the prioress bless herself and interestedly sit down in the bleakness farthest away from the postulant.

"What else?" Sister Léocadie asks.

Mariette thinks for a little while and says, "We are alone. We touch each other, but he withdraws. 'You are unclean,' he says, and I am ashamed because I see that it's true. Every sin I have committed is written in ink on my skin. Christ tells me to undress. And then he gently washes me with his hands. With holy water from great earthen jugs heated by the sun."

She pauses. She peers toward Mother Saint-Raphaël as if she's just learned that she's there.

Sister Geneviève flatly says, "We're in suspense, Mariette."

She continues, "We hear a hubbub and noise outside, as in an Eastern bazaar. Hands reach through the windows. Hopeless people walk in and then immediately walk out, as if the house is empty. What sorrow we both feel for them, but it's as if they can't see or hear us. We talk of a great many things, of affliction and faith and the full love of God. Everything he says is put so simply. Every word penetrates me as softly as water entering a sponge. Weeks seem to pass, and yet only a half-hour goes by. I know from hearing the choir singing the verses and responsories for Lauds. And he tells me what a great pleasure it is for his father to hear that. All our trying to please him pleases him, Jesus says."

She kneels just in front of the frowning prioress, her half-mittened hands nestled against her habit. She smiles. "And he gives me food as I have never eaten. And fine wine from a jeweled chalice. When he tells me to sleep, I do so at once, and he holds me. And I share in him as if he's inside me. And he is."

Mother Saint-Raphaël firmly purses her mouth and harshly slaps Mariette's face. And then she gets up and goes out.

Mass of Saint John of the Cross

Collation. A flame trembles in the palm of a used-up candle beside Sister Véronique as she reads the *Lectio Divina* of Saint Ignatius of Antioch's "Epistle to the Romans." And the prioress is drinking plain hot water as she peers across the nighted refectory at Mariette.

She seems hooded and dour and disoriented as she sits with her hands inside her sleeves, not eating, not hearing, hardly there at all. Everything seems dire to the postulant. Every choice seems taken from her. And then Mariette seems to perceive a call and she looks up into the darkness as she slips into another ecstasy, her healed hands rising up from her lap as if she's lifting an offertory, and then freezing there, high above the dining table, as if she's turned to wood.

Everyone stares at Mariette's trance until the prioress interrupts Sister Véronique's reading by irritably shouting, "Wake her!"

Sister Hermance puts down her spoon and tentatively touches Mariette twice.

"Harder."

She gives Mariette a fiercer push but she's firm as furniture to her hand and Sister Hermance appeals to the prioress with the shine of tears in her eyes.

The kitchen workers have come out and when Sister Saint-Léon theatrically kneels, five or six sisters join her.

Mother Saint-Raphaël stands and the hush of her sandals is the only sound as she walks over to the postulant and stares. "Look at me," the prioress says.

Mariette is still. She seldom breathes. Even in her eyes there is no travel.

Mother Saint-Raphaël picks up Mariette's unused fork and hears the sisters gasp as she tests a tine against Mariette's cheek.

She doesn't flinch.

Experimentally, the prioress scrawls the fork down Mariette's neck and hears the silence behind her as she presses harder on the habit until she is holding the fork threateningly against Mariette's left breast. She thinks about stabbing it to demonstrate her seriousness, but then thinks further and Mother Saint-Raphaël takes the fork away and silently prays for God's forgiveness as she turns to say the blessing after meals.

All the sisters then rise up and pray while Mariette stays as she was. All observe the blood dripping from her palms.

Mother Saint-Raphaël slowly walks to the hallway, but only a half-dozen sisters follow. She turns with great irritation and shouts, "*Christ* commands you to leave!"

Hands touch down in the blood covenant as the sisters pass out of the dining hall.

All through the night the Great Silence is torn.

Second rising.

Easy water rustles over stones beneath a Queen Anne's lace of ice.

Warmer, and a southerly breeze. Cathedrals of clouds just above the horizon.

Hurrying sandals in the hallway.

Choiring and starshine and trickling snow.

Mass of Saints Perpetua and Felicitas, Martyrs

Sister Sabine is on her haunches by a Guernsey cow, drilling hot milk into a tin pail. She props her head on the hide and prays to the blurred stain of blood on the back of her hand.

Sheep whose wool is tan as slush herd against the flitched boards of a fodder shed until Sister Saint-Luc walks out with a great load of cornstalks, a blood cross on her forehead. All follow her to the hurdle.

Dr. Claude Baptiste is in his Kashmir overcoat as he smokes his fifth cigarette of the morning and walks in the priest's yard just behind the high walls of the priory. Everywhere the snow seems blue. Eastward there is rain. Tilting his back into a poplar trunk, he follows a gray braid of smoke as it softly breaks against a tree limb and disappears. *Youth*, he thinks. *Trust. Faith. Ambition.* He hears kitchen noise, and then he hears the old priest falter out of his house and ask, "Shall we go then?"

Sister Aimée is hustling down the hallway toward the oratory and hesitating here and there to wait for Mariette, who walks without hurry and with great hurt, one white-bandaged hand touching its way along the high white wall, one hand tendering her left side.

Thirty sisters are lining up for Terce at the oratory doors and are trying not to dishonor the postulant with sudden prying, but Sister Honoré clenches her thick waist in her arms and frankly stares until Mariette hobbles by, and then the choirmistress unblanks her eyes and bluntly taps the castanets twice and the great doors open.

Sister Aimée has not prepared Mariette for the men in the prioress's suite. Père Marriott is sitting broodingly at the grand pecan desk in a fresh cassock, and he is as absent as an overcoat hung on a chair as he silently turns pages of Sister Marguerite's handwriting. And her father is there, too, in a pitch-black suit and vest and ankle-high shoes, putting

Sister Aimée's infirmary report in the bookcase, his wreath of dark hair trained with a floral pomade, a half-inch of cigarette seemingly forgotten between his fingers.

Elaborate rains lash at the windowpanes and dulled sunshine sketches reeds on the floor. Mother Saint-Raphaël heavily positions herself against the chintz pillows of the sofa and holds Mariette in a hostile glare as Sister Aimée walks in with a hand towel and china bowl and pitcher, and puts them on a sill.

Warily skirting his eyes from Mariette, Dr. Baptiste sucks hard on the cigarette and kills it in a half-filled water glass while saying, "She'll have to take off her clothes."

Everything goes unsaid for a while. Mariette hides her hands in her sleeves and hoards her modesty until she asks, "Are you trying to turn it into a disease?"

Mother Saint-Raphaël says, "We have no competence in these matters. We have been like a household with a hundred opinions about an illness but no certainty. We need the verdict of a doctor. We need to be convinced that there is no natural explanation for these wonderful phenomena. When there is no other alternative, then perhaps we shall call them miraculous."

"We are only here to see," Père Marriott assures Mariette. "We shall try to be indifferent and serene, untroubled by whatever facts we turn up and friendly to whatever deductions those facts provide."

Mariette steps out of one roped sandal and the other and then takes off the stockings that hide her foot bandagings. Père Marriott gets up with difficulty and stands at a flecked and fractured window in order to give her privacy, but Dr. Baptiste washes his hands in the china bowl and skeptically peers at Mariette as she peels the headscarf away from her tangling brown hair. She gazes out at the wings of rain in flight across the horse paddock as she unties the cincture and gets out of her habit, and turns to her father in her nakedness. "*Je vous en prie*," she says. At your service.

Her father turns the trick card of his smile as he stares at her and dries his palms, then tosses the hand towel aside and walks up to Mariette. She blushes in humiliation as she feels his hand and his right thumb bluntly stroking the rib just beneath her left breast. She hears him say to Sister Aimée and Mother Saint-Raphaël, "You'll see there is no 'hand-width laceration.' Even no scarring."

Each of them is hushed for a moment and Dr. Baptiste takes Mariette's left wrist in his hand and stares into her flashing eyes. Without looking away, he says, "Have you scissors, Sister Aimée?"

She gives him a pair and he begins roughly cutting through the hand bandages.

Underneath is blood as thick as a red wax seal. Touching its hardness with great curiosity, her father asks, "Does that hurt?"

She flinches but doesn't say.

Dr. Baptiste turns to the priest, but he seems to be in prayer, so he hesitantly says to Mother Saint-Raphaël, "And now what I'll have to do is tear just a bit of this away. Like a child picks a scab."

"Yes," she says. "You may proceed."

"Try water," Mariette says.

"Excuse me?" he says.

She walks away from him and past Sister Aimée to the china bowl where he'd washed his hands, and she presses hers underwater and holds them there. Tears blur her eyes at the hot sting of pain as the blood feebly unplaits and swims, and then she lifts up her hands again.

Dr. Baptiste goes over and interestedly picks up a hand towel and hastily scrubs her left palm. And he is pleased as he commands the old priest to look.

Père Marriott hunches over her hands in the half-light. He urgently finds his brass-rimmed eyeglasses and holds them up and peers at her hands again. The blood and the holes have disappeared.

She tells him, "Christ took back the wounds."

She expects her father to stare at her with fear and astonishment, but he is, as always, frank and unimpressed, as firm and practical as a clock. "And your feet?" he asks.

"I have no wounds."

"Even that is miraculous!" Père Marriott says.

Dr. Baptiste smirks at him and then at Mother Saint-Raphaël. "You all have been duped."

The priest insists, "Explain it to them!"

Mariette flatly says, "What God freely gave me has just as freely been taken away."

"Christ talks to her," her father says. "The Devil strikes her when she tries to pray. She is always saying preposterous things; that's why we don't get along."

She turns to Mother Saint-Raphaël and says, "Whatever I told you was true," but the prioress frowns at her in the fullness of sorrow and says, "You disappoint me, Mariette."

Sister Aimée folds the hand towels and hurriedly takes away the china bowl.

"Shall I go now?" Dr. Baptiste asks.

Mother Saint-Raphaël's face is hidden behind her hand when she answers. "Yes, Doctor. Thank you. We have investigated this quite enough." And then she says, "You stay, Mariette."

When she and the postulant are alone, Mother Saint-Raphaël shifts a chintz pillow and pats a sofa cushion beside her. She stares impassively at Mariette as she sits. She says, "That was simply political, what I said—that you disappoint me. I personally believe that what you say happened did indeed happen. We could never prove it, of course. Skeptics will always prevail. God gives us just enough to seek him, and never enough to fully find him. To do more would inhibit our freedom, and our freedom is very dear to God."

Mariette is trying not to cry, but she can feel her mouth tremble as she asks, "Are you sending me away?"

"Yes. We are."

"I have always dreamed . . ."

She is stilled when the prioress touches her knee. Mother Saint-Raphaël tells her, "God sometimes wants our desire for a religious vocation but not the deed itself." She then gets up with difficulty and gives half her weight to her cane. "I'll go get Sister Agnès."

Endless rains make a garden of the window glass, reeds and herbs and periwinkles. Mariette sketches them with a nail as she dismally looks outside, and then she hears the door open and sees Sister Agnès in the hallway. "I'll just be getting your things," she says.

Mariette says nothing. She simply waits like an intricate memory as Sister Agnès heavily backs into the room hauling a ship's trunk along the floor. And then Mariette again gets into Mrs. Baptiste's wedding gown of white Holland cloth and watered silk.

"You're still lovely," Sister Agnès says.

"Thank you."

Sister Agnès grins at her. "I'm the first to get you girls when you join us, and I'm the one you go to when you're getting out. Hatched by me; dispatched by me. I'm an important person here."

"You are."

"We were talking about it, Sister Zélie and me. You put one over on us."

Mariette angles her head and snags an ivory comb through her hair. She twinges and holds her hand.

"Are you hurt, dear?"

"Christ let me keep the pain."

Sister Agnès gazes at her. She thinks without a path. She finally says, "Your father's in the priest's house. Waiting."

"Well, good-bye," Mariette says.

"We aren't but just a few of us fit to stay here."

"Well, you've all been very kind," she says.

"You think so? Even now?"

"Oh yes," she says. "You let God use you."

She goes into the oratory and genuflects toward Christ in the tabernacle before unlatching the door in the oaken grille and walking out to the high altar, where she genuflects again. She sees Sister Catherine ironing a Lenten chasuble in the sacristy, but she doesn't speak. She passes through the Communion railing and in solemn procession walks out of the Church of Our Lady of Sorrows, just as she entered it in August.

And then she is bleakly tottering through the churned slush and mud of the village, her hair in torrents, wintry rain like tines on her face, the white Holland cloth soaked through and hedged with stains. She falls to her hands and knees and just stays there until she sees a frightened girl in a seal coat on a house porch with the noon mail in her hands. The girl makes the sign of the cross as she kneels, and Mariette forlornly gets to her feet and goes forward to her father's house.

Mass of Saint Thomas Aquinas, Confessor

Mariette puts a houseplant on the sill of a dining room window as children hurry by after school. She sees the children hesitate and stare. She smiles gently but withdraws.

Mass of Saint Francesca of Rome, Widow

She goes into the rooms upstairs, getting used to them again. She stands in the book and paper chaos of her father's dark-paneled den. Whiskey is in a square crystal decanter. A tumbler is turned upside down on a handkerchief. She chooses a green chintz chair to sit on, resting her wrists atop antimacassars, her heeled shoes paired as if in a store. She prays until God is there.

Mass of Saint Lucy, Virgin, Martyr. 1912

She's in a housedress and washing dishes at the kitchen sink as a high school boy she's tutoring sits on a stool at a pantry table and tries sentences in his notebook.

She peers outside. The skies are dark. White flakes are fluttering through the trees like torn paper. And yet it is still warm enough that she can hear water trickle under its gray crepe of ice.

She asks him, "Are you ready?"

"I think so."

She sponges a milk glass. "Whom are you looking for?"

The boy hunches over his handwriting and reads, "*Qui est-ce que vous cherchez?*"

"Excellent. And now: What are you waiting for?"

He hunts his answer. "*Qu'est-ce que vous attendez?*"

"*Très bien,*" Mariette says. And then she holds her hands against her apron as if she's suddenly in pain. She cringes and hangs there for a long time, and then the hurt subsides.

She hears him get up from his stool. "Are you okay?" he asks.

She blushes when she turns to him. She tells him, "Yes. Of course."

Mass of Saint Martha, Virgin. 1917

Dr. Baptiste tilts heavily in his wheelchair in the shaded green yard, his dinner napkin still tucked in his high starched collar, as Mariette walks from the heat of the house with a Japanese tea service on a tray. She puts it on his side table and he pours for himself as she sits in a striped canvas chair. "Would you like some?" he asks.

She smiles and shakes her head no. She takes off her shoes.

"We'll be having tomatoes soon," he says.

Wrens are flying in and out of the trees. She shades her eyes as she looks at the great orange sun going down. She looks at its haul of shadows.

"We'll have tomato Provençale," he says. "And Creole style. With curry." Dr. Baptiste hears only silence from her. And then he hears Mariette as she softly whispers the *Nunc Dimittis* of Compline.

Mass of Saint Thérèse of Lisieux. 1929

She stands before an upright floor mirror at forty and skeins hair that is half gray. She pouts her mouth. She esteems her full breasts as she has seen men esteem them. She haunts her milk-white skin with her hands.

Even this I have given you.

Mass of the Conversion of Saint Paul, Apostle. 1933

She kneels just inside the Church of Our Lady of Sorrows, behind the pews of holy old women half sitting with their rosaries, their heads hooded in black scarves. High Mass has ended. Externs are putting out the candles and vacuuming the carpets. And then there is silence, and she opens to Saint Paul: "We are afflicted in every way possible, but we are not crushed; full of doubts, we never despair. We are persecuted but never abandoned; we are struck down but never destroyed. Continually we carry about in our bodies the dying of Jesus, so that in our bodies the life of Jesus may also be revealed."

Easter Vigil, 1937

Dearest Mother Philomène,
You are so kind to remember me in your letter and your prayers! And what marvelous news that you've been chosen the new prioress. God surely had a hand in it, as he has in all the decisions there in that holiest of places.

Yes, it has indeed been thirty years. Are we such crones as that? I so often think of you and Sister Hermance and the others. Whenever I can get to Vespers, I try to hear your voices, and I sigh theatrically and think how glorious it would be to be with you there again.

I still pray the hours and honor the vows and go to a sunrise

Mass. (Each day I thank God for the Chrysler automobile, though I hate the noise.) I tidy the house and tend the garden and have dinner with the radio on. Even now I look out at a cat huddled down in the adder's fern, at a fresh wind nagging the sheets on the line, at hills like a green sea in the east and just beyond them the priory, and the magnificent puzzle is, for a moment, solved, and God is there before me in the being of all that is not him.

And yet sometimes I am so sad. Even when I have friends over often for tea or canasta, there is a Great Silence here for weeks and weeks, and the Devil tells me the years since age seventeen have been a great abeyance and I have been like a troubled bride pining each night for a husband who is lost without a trace.

Children stare in the grocery as if they know ghostly stories about me, and I hear the hushed talk when I hobble by or lose the hold in my hands, but Christ reminds me, as he did in my greatest distress, that he loves me more, now that I am despised, than when I was so richly admired in the past.

And Christ still sends me roses. We try to be formed and held and kept by him, but instead he offers us freedom. And now when I try to know his will, his kindness floods me, his great love overwhelms me, and I hear him whisper, Surprise me.

Notes on the Authors

FREDERICK BUECHNER (b. 1926) is a writer of fiction and nonfiction whose works explore spiritual subjects. A Presbyterian minister, he taught religion for many years at Phillips Exeter Academy. He now lives in southern Vermont.

JOHN L'HEUREUX (b. 1934) is a poet, novelist, and short story writer. "The Expert on God" is from his short story collection *Comedians*, published in 1990.

GABRIEL GARCÍA MÁRQUEZ (b. 1928), a Colombian novelist and journalist, was awarded the Nobel Prize for literature in 1982. "The Saint" appeared in *Strange Pilgrims*, his 1992 short story collection.

RAYMOND CARVER (1939–1988), a native of the Pacific Northwest, was one of the most accomplished short story writers of the second half of this century. His work is known for its focus on introspection and discovery in the lives of working-class men and women.

FLANNERY O'CONNOR (1925–1964), among the most important writers of the American South, was profoundly influenced in her novels and short stories by her Roman Catholic beliefs. Her writing is concerned with matters of faith and grace, and with the violence that she felt often surrounded them.

BERNARD MALAMUD (1914-1986) was born in Brooklyn, and has written numerous short stories and novels, including *The Fixer*, for which he received a Pulitzer Prize and his second National Book Award.

FRANCINE PROSE (b. 1947) has written eight novels (including her 1981 book *Household Saints*), two collections of short stories, and many essays and reviews. She lives near Woodstock, New York.

RICHARD BAUSCH (b. 1945), has written six novels and three collections of short stories. Twice he has received the National Magazine Award for his stories. "Design" appeared in his 1990 collection *The Fireman's Wife and Other Stories*. Bausch lives in Virginia.

HANNAH GREEN (b. 1926) is the author of *The Dead of the House*, published in 1972. *Golden Spark, Little Soul*, from which the passage here is excerpted, will be published in three volumes by Random House. She lives in New York City, and has spent part of every year since 1977 in Conques, France, home of the statue of Sainte Foy.

ALICE WALKER (b. 1944) won an American Book Award and a Pulitzer Prize for her 1982 novel *The Color Purple*. "The Welcome Table" is from her collection *In Love and Trouble: Stories of Black Women*.

RON HANSEN (b. 1947), a writer who lives and teaches in California, received an Award in Literature from the American Academy and Institute of Arts and Letters for his 1989 short story collection *Nebraska*. His novel *Mariette in Ecstasy* was published in 1991.
